Foundations of Christian Music:

The Music of Pre-Constantinian Christianity

by Edward Foley

Capuchin-Franciscan of the Province of St. Joseph
Teaching on the Faculty at Chicago's Catholic Theological Union

THE ALCUIN CLUB and the GROUP FOR RENEWAL OF WORSHIP (GROW)

The Alcuin Club, which exists to promote the study of Christian liturgy in general and of Anglican liturgy in particular, traditionally published a single volume annually for its members. This ceased in 1986 but is resuming in 1992. Similarly, GROW was responsible from 1975 to 1986 for the quarterly 'Grove Liturgical Studies'. Since the beginning of 1987 the two have sponsored a Joint Editorial Board to produce quarterly 'Joint Liturgical Studies', details of which are to be found at the end of this Study along with details of their separate publications.

THE COVER PICTURE

shows a detail of Jewish musical instruments from the Arch of Titus in Rome.

First Impression September 1992
ISSN 0951-2667
ISBN 1 85174 218 2

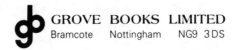
GROVE BOOKS LIMITED
Bramcote   Nottingham   NG9 3DS

CONTENTS

ACKNOWLEDGEMENT

I wish to thank Robin Faulkner for her help in reproducing the plans of the various buildings which are printed on pages 27, 39, 53 and 71 below.

ABBREVIATIONS

EJ   *Encyclopaedia Judaica*. eds. Cecil Roth and Geoffrey Wigoder. 16 vols. (Keter Publishing House, Jerusalem, 1972).

IDB   *The Interpreter's Dictionary of the Bible*. ed. George Buttrick, *et al.* 4 vols. (Abingdon, New York-Nashville, 1962).

Mishnah   all translations from *The Mishnah*. trans. Jacob Neusner. (Yale University Press, New Haven-London, 1988).

NGDMM   *New Groves Dictionary of Music and Musicians*. ed. Stanley Sadie. 20 vols. (W. W. Norton, New York, 1980).

NJBC   *The New Jerome Biblical Commentary*. eds. Raymond Brown, Joseph Fitzmyer and Roland Murphy (Prentice Hall, Englewood Cliffs, New Jersey, 1988).

NTA   *New Testament Apocrypha*. eds. Edgar Hennecke and Wilhelm Schneemelcher. 2 vols. trans. R. McL. Wilson (Westminster Press, Philadelphia, 1976).

TDNT   *Theological Dictionary of the New Testament*. eds. Gerhard Kittel and Gerhard Friedrich. trans. Geoffrey W. Bromiley. 10 vols. (Wm. Eerdmans, Grand Rapids, 1964).

Introduction

For the student of liturgical music, the search for an adequate overview of Christian worship music in the first three centuries of the common era can be a daunting experience. There are many fine surveys of Church music, but few of them give much attention to the time before Constantine (d. 337). While there are numerous particular studies on various musical texts, practices or personalities in the early Christian community, these seldom supply an adequate picture of the basic trends in early Christian worship or its music.

The reasons for this lacuna are multiple. The sources about worship in the first three centuries of the common era are quite fragmentary. There was little concern among the early believers to document their cultic or musical practices for latter generations. What sources we do have provide little specific information about music, or contain information that is often allegorical and difficult to interpret. More problematic than the sources is the very question about the nature of music within emerging Christianity.

In order for the contemporary inquirer to understand the music of pre-Constantinian Christianity it is necessary to think cross-culturally. The first Christians lived in a world very different from our own: a world dissimilar not only in time and geography, but distinctive in the ways that its inhabitants perceived and talked about reality. Any attempt to understand early Christian worship music, therefore, requires more than simply learning a new vocabulary or developing an ability to reconcile divergent texts about music in the ancient world. Rather, it compels us to think differently about music and its relationship to ritual. In doing so we will discover that some contemporary categories—such as distinctions between music and speech—are anachronistic frameworks that the ancients did not employ. Furthermore, many contemporary practices, such as our ability to celebrate worship without music, would be completely unintelligible to Christians of the first centuries. In order to enter into the world of early Christianity and comprehend the place and function of music in that world, we have to imagine and penetrate an auditory environment very different from our own.

Although there are many aspects of this ancient auditory environment that deserve our attention, none is more critical to the current study than the role of sound phenomena in divine revelation and worship. While contemporary Western society is visually oriented and believes what it sees, the first followers of Jesus—like their Jewish forebears—lived in a world where hearing was believing. Whether the interchange was a human affair or a divine-human dialogue, sound events were the prime mediator of presence and truth. This aural way of knowing deeply influenced the tonal landscape of early Christian worship which was as much a sonic as an optic event.

---

[1] 'Fullness': the Syriac can also mean 'completion, fulfilling, satisfying.'

Before asking specific questions about early Christian music, therefore, we will first explore the tonal landscape of ancient Judaism and the New Testament world. This investigation will provide the necessary context for raising specific questions about 'music' in early Christianity. After this preliminary investigation we will consider specific 'musical' aspects of early Christian worship.

While there are many ways in which to organize such an investigation, we have chosen to organize the material according to the various places or types of places in which the followers of Jesus worshipped. We will begin with the Temple of Herod and then the synagogues of the first century, followed by a consideration of the borrowed spaces that characterized emerging Christianity in the first century CE, and finally the house churches of the second and third centuries. In each chapter we will describe the setting, and then attempt to answer questions about the type of 'musicians' that functioned in that setting, the texts that might have been sung there, the manner of performing those texts, and the place of instruments in the worship. A brief summary will conclude each chapter.

Although there is much we do not know about the role of music in the emerging Christian community, there is an abundance of references, reconstructions and hypotheses about the music of this era in the literature. There is no way that this slim volume can do justice to all of this material. Rather, what follows is intended as a guide to the central questions about the role of music in the emerging Christian community, as well as a credible survey of key primary and secondary sources about early Christian 'music'. Such historical considerations are foundational for those who wrestle with contemporary issues of liturgical music, and who need to befriend the tradition in order to respond adequately to the challenge of sung worship.

1. The Auditory Environment[1]

While there are numerous ways in which to characterize societies of various ages, in terms of communication it is possible to divide cultures 'into three successive stages: (1) oral or oral-aural, (2) script . . . and (3) electronic.'[2] The fundamental distinction between stages one and two—between an oral and what might be called a proto-literate society—is that the former does not use any form of phonetic writing.[3] While an alphabet is not the only system which allows for phonetic transcription,[4] the presence of an alphabetic system does signal that a society has at least begun the transition out of its oral stage.

For those who wish to understand the nature of an oral society, Walter Ong offers an important caution: 'the differences between oral-aural culture and our own technological culture are . . . so vast and so profound as to defy total itemization.'[5] These differences are underscored by Ong's own limited itemization of some of the characteristics of an oral society, in which explanation is possible only by drawing negative parallels with contemporary experience. For example, Ong suggests that 'one of the most striking and informative differences between an oral culture and our own is that an oral-aural culture is necessarily a culture with a relationship to time different from ours.' In developing this concept, Ong relies almost exclusively on negative parallels to make his point: '[An oral-aural culture] has no records. It does have memory, but this is not by any means the same as records, for the written record is not a remembrance but an aid to recall. It does not belong to us as memory does. It is an external thing.'[6]

---

[1] 'Auditory environment' and 'acoustic environment' are terms that are meant to demonstrate a concern not simply or essentially for an individual sound or musical event, but for the physical, historical and cultural environment than shapes the perception and understanding of such individual sounds or musical events. The terms are somewhat analogous to those of 'soundscape' or 'sonic environment' coined by F. Murray Schafer. See, for example, the definitions Schafer offers in his glossary of *The Tuning of the World* (Alfred Knopf, New York, 1977), pp.274-75, and *passim*.

[2] Walter Ong, *The Presence of the Word* (Yale University Press, New Haven, 1967), p.17; Havelock offers a refinement on this three-part schema by suggesting that the first stage of a culture in communication terms is that of primary orality, followed by the proto-literate, the craft-literate, the semi-literate, and the fully literate stages. (Eric Havelock, *The Muse Learns to Write: Reflections on Orality and Literacy from Antiquity to the Present* (Yale University Press, New Haven-London, 1986), p.65).

[3] Although the common use of the term 'writing' as applied to any and every form of symbolization without distinction blurs the boundaries between the various stages of a society's development, Havelock, *The Muse learns to Write*, p.65.

[4] Jack Goody, *The Interface between the Written and the Oral* (Cambridge University Press, 1987), pp.38-41.

[5] Ong, *The Presence of the Word*, p. 23.

[6] *Ibid.*

Havelock proposes that one way to recognize the difference between our culture and an oral culture is by recognizing that in primary orality, relationships between human beings are governed exclusively by acoustics. He elaborates: 'The psychology of such relationships is . . . acoustics. The relation between an individual and his society is acoustic, between himself and his tradition, his law, his government. To be sure, primary communication begins visually with the smile, the frown, the gesture. But these do not get us very far. Recognition, response, thought itself, occur when we hear linguistic sounds and melodies and ourselves respond to them, as we utter a variant set of sounds to amend or amplify or negate what we have heard.'[1] While there are many other features of an oral society that one could enumerate[2], this initial foray into cautions and characteristics alerts us to the radical differences between contemporary technological culture and the world of the ancient Near East.

ORALITY IN ANCIENT ISRAEL

In order for us to grasp something of the acoustic environment of ancient Israel we need to sketch in general terms when Israel was at the stage of primary orality and when, with the introduction of an alphabet and writing, it moved to the proto-literate stage. This necessitates the briefest of historical introductions to ancient Israel, followed by a similarly abbreviated overview of the history of alphabetic script in ancient Israel. These sketches will provide us with a framework for discussing the rise of writing within Israel, the movement from oral to written prophecy in Israel, the continuance of what might be termed 'residual orality' in ancient Israel as it developed into a literate society, and allow some general comments about the dynamic nature of Hebrew language and thought. These historical-cultural reflections will allow us to gauge the auditory environment in Palestine in the first centuries of the Common Era at the birth of Christianity.

---

[1] Havelock, *The Muse learns to Write*, pp.65-66.
[2] The following list is distilled from Ong, *Presence of the Word*, pp.22-35 and Havelock, *The Muse Learns to Write*, pp.63-78: 1) in an oral society communication, even between individuals, has an aspect of social phenomenon; 2) oral societies rely on the narrative format for memorizing and transmitting fundamental truths; 3) tradition is taught by action, not by idea or principle; 4) the oral audience participates not merely by listening passively but by active participation—they clap, dance and sing collectively in response to the chanting of the singer; 5) an oral society has no history in the modern sense of that term; 6) an oral society nourishes memory skills beyond those cultivated in present-day technological societies; 7) in oral societies ritualization becomes the means of memorization; and 8) in oral societies words are more celebrations and less tools than in literate cultures. For a cautionary note on comparing literate to non-literate societies, see Ruth Finnegan, 'Literacy versus Non-literacy: The Great Divide?' in *Modes of Thought: Essays on Thinking in Western and Non-Western Societies*, eds. Robin Horton & Ruth Finnegan (Faber & Faber, London, 1973), pp.112-144.

An **Historical Framework:** The history of Israel[1] commonly begins with the Patriarchal period, which de Vaux suggests can be roughly dated to the first half of the second millennium BCE.[2] A second phase of Israel's early history is connected to the sojourn in Egypt and Joseph's rise to power (Gen 37-50).[3] A third phase encompasses the Exodus and Conquest events. The former, possibly involving two separate exoduses[4], can be dated in the middle of the 13th century BCE. The latter—which was as much a period of coexistence, peaceful infiltration and interdependence between the residents of Canaan with the Hebrew settlers as it was a time of conquest[5]—spanned the period slightly before the exodus(es) until the mid-eleventh century BCE. The latter part of the period of the Conquest is roughly co-terminous with the age of the Judges. By the middle of the eleventh century BCE a series of cultural and political developments gave rise to the monarchy in Israel. At the death of Solomon (922 BCE) the kingdom was divided. The northern kingdom (Israel) fell to Assyria in 721 BCE; the southern kingdom (Judah) fell to Babylon in 587 BCE.

A schematic of this history follows:

Patriarchal Period	ca. 2000-1700 BCE
Sojourn in Egypt	ca. 1700-1300 BCE?
entry of Semitic groups into Egypt	
the Joseph Story	
Exodus and 'Conquest'	ca. 1300-1050 BCE
the exodus(es)	ca. 1250 BCE
the 'conquest'	ca. 1300-1050 BCE
Age of the Judges	ca. 1200-1050 BCE
Monarchy	ca. 1020-587 BCE
division of kingdom	922 BCE
fall of the Northern kingdom	721 BCE
fall of the Southern kingdom	587 BCE
the Exile	587-539 BCE

---

[1] See the accessible outline by Addison Wright and Roland Murphy in *NJBC* 75:5-144; this outline provides the basis for the historical reconstruction which follows.

[2] Roland de Vaux, *The Early History of Israel*, trans. David Smith (Westminster Press, Philadelphia, 1978), p.266.

[3] While it appears that certain Semitic groups entered Egypt sometime in the middle of the second millennium BCE, the historicity of the Joseph story is disputed. See, for example, Siegfried Herrmann, *A History of Israel in Old Testament Times*, 2nd ed. (Fortress, Philadelphia, 1981), p.56.

[4] de Vaux, *The Early History of Israel*, pp. 363-387.

[5] See, for example, David Noel Freedman and David Graf, eds. *Palestine in Transition*, The Social World of Biblical Antiquity, series editor James W. Flanagan (Almond Press, Sheffield, 1983): especially Marvin L. Chaney, 'Ancient Palestinian Peasant Movements and the Formation of Premonarchic Israel', pp.39-90.

The Alphabet and Writing in Ancient Israel: It is possible that a Semitic alphabet[1] could have appeared as early as 1900 BCE.[2] The earliest extant Semitic texts are Proto-Canaanite, dating from the seventeenth century BCE, from the region now known as Syria.[3] Proto-Canaanite and Canaanite scripts were succeeded by Old Phoenician (or North Semitic) script in the eleventh century BCE. The Israelites borrowed either a Phoenician or a similar Palestinian script (a sub-species of Proto-Canaanite)—employed in Palestine before their arrival— sometime after the thirteenth century BCE.[4] Written Hebrew, properly speaking, has a single witness from the eleventh century BCE, and many more by the eighth century BCE.[5]

A schematic of this history[6] follows:

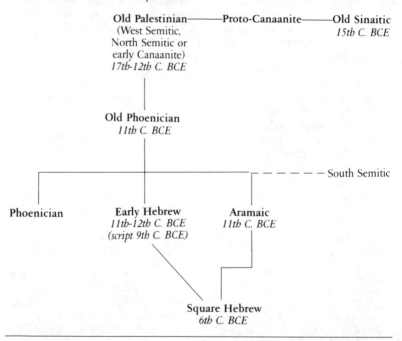

Old Palestinian————Proto-Canaanite————Old Sinaitic
(West Semitic, *15th C. BCE*
North Semitic or
early Canaanite)
17th-12th C. BCE

Old Phoenician
11th C. BCE

————————————————— South Semitic

Phoenician   Early Hebrew   Aramaic
                  11th-12th C. BCE *11th C. BCE*
                  (script 9th C. BCE)

Square Hebrew
6th C. BCE

---

[1] These were what Goody calls 'consonantal alphabets' in counter-distinction to alphabets consisting of consonants and vowels, which did not appear until around 750 BCE in Greece (Goody, pp.40-41).

[2] B. L. Ullman, *Ancient Writing and Its Influence*, Medieval Academy Reprints for Teaching 10 (University of Toronto Press, Toronto, 1980 [1932]), p.11.

[3] Goody, p.41.

[4] Goody, pp.43 and 45.

[5] Goody, p.45.

[6] This schematic is distilled from Goody's more complex table on the genealogy of the alphabet (Goody, Table 2, p.48).

A comparison of this schematic with the preceding historical sketch suggests that writing entered the history of Israel very early. A first step in this process was a borrowing of either a Phoenician or a similar Palestinian script from the Canaanites, probably in the twelfth or eleventh century BCE. It is no coincidence that the refinement of Israel's national identity, symbolized in the rise of the monarchy, occurred in exactly the same period from which we have the first exemplars of Hebrew inscriptions.[1] It is possible that, just as guilds of professional scribes existed in Egypt and Mesopotamia at this time[2], so did the emerging monarchy borrow this element of statecraft from Egyptian or Canaanite governmental models.[3] The emergence of Israel as a nation is intimately related to the emergence of the Hebrew language itself.

Writing, Scribalism and the Deuteronomistic Movement: From the Old Testament we learn how widespread writing was among the Israelites. As de Vaux summarizes,

'Writing was in common use at an early date. Besides the professional scribes, like those employed at the court for administration (2 Sam. 8.17; 20.25; 1 Kgs. 4.3, etc.), and private secretaries like Baruch (Jer. 36.4), members of the ruling class could write, judging by the stories of Jezabel (1 Kgs. 21.8) and of Isaiah (Isa. 8.1). But these were not the only ones: a young man of Sukkoth was able to give Gideon, in writing, the names of all the chiefs of his clan (Judg. 8.14), and the commandment of Deut. 6.9; 11.20 presumed that every head of a family could write).'[4]

While writing entered Israel's history early, it did not serve as a primary means of communication or a central vehicle for the development of new theologies in ancient Israel. Thus, while sections of the Pentateuch were put into writing in the tenth century BCE[5], these elements did not originate as written texts and retained what might be called a residual orality.[6] This situation began to change, however, in the seventh century BCE.

In the eighth and seventh centuries BCE Assyria was a major military force in the Near East, dominating both the Northern and Southern Kingdoms. Under

---

[1] The Afeg Tablet from the eleventh century, and the Gezer Calendar, probably of the late tenth century, the Davidic period. Goody, p.45.

[2] Normal K. Gottwald, *The Hebrew Bible* (Fortress Press, Philadelphia, 1985), pp.567-568.

[3] Joseph McIntyre, 'Jeremiah 36 and the Emergence of Scribal Prophecy'—unpublished MA Thesis (Catholic Theological Union, Chicago, 1990), p.10.

[4] Roland de Vaux, *Ancient Israel*, 2 vols. (McGraw-Hill, New York-Toronto, 1965), 1:49.

[5] i.e. the J tradition; see Raymond Brown's chronology of approximate dates of the collection of composition of the works of the Old Testament in the *NJBC* 66:23.

[6] Walter Ong defines residual orality as 'habits of thought and expression . . . deriving from the dominance of the oral as a medium in a given culture'. *Rhetoric, Romance and Technology* (Cornell University Press, Ithaca NY, 1971), pp.27-28.

the influence of the Assyrian empire, which greatly valued the role of the professional scribe,[1] scribalism flourished throughout Near East to the extent that this is sometimes characterized as a 'scribal age'.[2] In Israel this trend came to fruition in the emergence of the Deuteronomistic movement:

'It is hardly coincidental that the Deuteronomistic movement arose within this period. The written incorporation of historical traditions and legal codes by Deuteronomists parallels this increasingly prominent role of the scribe. This is evident in the Biblical portrayal of the Josianic Reform, which symbolizes the Deuteronomistic movement itself (2 Kgs. 22). Here, it is the *written* word that is the basis for the king's conversion. Likewise, it is a scribe—Shaphan—who is accorded a primary place in the discovery (22.3), the handling (22.8) and the interpretation (22.14) of the scroll. From this point on the written traditions will be an increasingly important component in the cultic life of Jerusalem.'[3]

While the Deuteronomists are pivotal for giving written shape to the law, their influence on proto-literate Israel extends further, into prophetic literature. It is this development which becomes determinative for identifying the Word of God with the written word in ancient Israel.

From Oral to Written Prophecy: Around the time of the Deuteronomistic movement a revolution was taking place in prophetic literature.[4] As M. B. Dick suggests, this revolution entailed the increased incorporation of written passages in prophecy, which in essence and origin was an oral medium. This conclusion is based on R. Coote's work on the Book of Amos[5] which demonstrated that one strata of Amos (Amos A) reflected the existence of orally delivered oracles while a second strata of the book (Amos B) suggested prophecy that was never orally delivered but was a written composition. Dick concludes that, because of the resemblance of Amos B to the Deuteronomist, it can be dated to the late seventh century.[6]

The work of the prophet Jeremiah stands at a pivotal moment in the transition from oral to written prophecy. Jeremiah 36 describes the production of a written prophetic document.[7] What is unusual in this account, however, is that the process of oral prophecy and scribal transmission—separate processes in the

---

[1] The Assyrian monarch Asshurbanipal (668-626 BCE), for example, not only employed numerous scribes and assembled an impressive library, but himself mastered the art of writing (James Mullenberg, 'Baruch the Scribe' in *Proclamation and Presence* (John Knox Press, Richmond, 1970), p.216).

[2] *Ibid.*, p.217.

[3] McIntyre, p.11.

[4] M. B. Dick, 'Prophetic *Poie-sis* and the Verbal Icon' in *Catholic Biblical Quarterly* 46 (1984) 230.

[5] R. B. Coote, *Amos Among the Prophets: Composition and Theology* (Fortress Press, Philadelphia, 1981).

[6] Dick, p.230.

[7] McIntyre, p.4; the following analysis of the role of Jeremiah is reliant upon McIntyre's work.

previously described Book of Amos—now appear to converge. 'Either during his lifetime or shortly thereafter, Jeremiah's oracles, and the accounts of many incidents within his life, were committed to writing.'[1] While the reasons for this convergence are yet to be agreed upon, the result of this process is that the written word is identified with the word of the Lord.[2]

By the post-exilic period, prophecy is more and more a written endeavour.[3] Dick suggests that the Book of Chronicles provides a *terminus ad quem* for this transition. 'By the time of the Chronicler, a contemporary of Haggai and Zechariah (ca. 520 BCE), prophecy was already presumed to be written.'[4]

Residual Orality in Ancient Israel: The appearance of a Hebrew alphabet, the rise of scribalism and the convergence of oral prophecy and scribal transmission in Jeremiah all attest to the gradual transformation of ancient Israel from a proto-literate to a craft- or even semi-literate society. Even the dominance of written prophecy in post-exilic Israel, however, does not mean the end of Israel as an oral society, for the transition from one stage of orality to another takes centuries to achieve.[5] Thus, while writing might have been widespread among the Israelites before the exile, de Vaux himself—who treats writing within the larger framework of education—concludes that most teaching was done by word of mouth.[6]

It was not only education that maintained an 'auditory bias' in ancient Israel. Many of the characteristics of this pre-literate state endured for centuries. The primary source for discovering these characteristics is the Old Testament. While it is true that the Old Testament was redacted by a society at least at the stage of craft-literacy, the texts themselves exhibit what Havelock calls 'concealed oralism'.[7] As he explains, concealed oralism is a way of acknowledging that 'genuine echoes from a primary orality long forgotten have been retained intermittently in a text otherwise devoted to revising them, epitomizing them, and incorporating them in a theological framework devised by a written tradition.'[8] While there are a number of indicators of this 'concealed oralism' in the Old Testament, a brief consideration of three of them should make the point.

---

[1] McIntyre, p.5.

[2] McIntyre hypothesizes, 'oral cultures seem to be uncertain about how to treat written documents ... it is evident that Jeremiah 36 is intended to resolve that question. It seems to address the theological issue of preserving a written tradition... I contend that the final form of Jeremiah 36 resolves this situation. It identifies the word of the Lord with the written word of Jeremiah.' (McIntyre, pp.47-48).

[3] Dick, *passim*.

[4] Dick, pp.230-231.

[5] Havelock, *The Muse learns to write*. In a related comment, Ruth Finnegan notes, 'In practice, interaction between oral and written forms is extremely common, and the idea that the use of writing *automatically* deals a death blow to oral literary forms has nothing to support it.' (*Oral Poetry: Its Nature, Significance and Social Context* (University Press, Cambridge, 1977), p.160).

[6] de Vaux, *Ancient Israel* 1:49.

[7] Havelock, *The Music learns to Write*, p.47.

[8] Havelock, *The Muse learns to Write*, p.47; Werner Kelber makes a similar assertion when he suggests that 'The objectifying, controlling power of the written medium, while taking the life out of spoken language, can freeze oral forms and preserve them in fossilized profiles.' (*The Oral and the Written Gospel* (Fortress Press, Philadelphia, 1983), p.44).

1). *The Dominance of Auditory over Visual Imagery in Divine Manifestations:* It is generally true that auditory images dominate the stories of divine manifestation in the Old Testament. This can be demonstrated in a number of ways.

First, there is what might be called the preparatory nature of the visual manifestation of God in the Old Testament. As Kittel notes, accounts of seeing God in the Hebrew Scriptures simply provide the setting for the revelation of the word that follows as, for example, in the vision of the prophet Isaiah (6.1ff) or Ezekiel (1.1ff). 'When God appears, it is not for the sake of the theophany, but in order ... to cause Himself to be heard indirectly or directly. The decisive religious statement is: "Hear the Word of the Lord" (Isa. 1.10; Jer. 2.4; Amos 7.16).'[1]

Second, the divine presence is often visually obscured, so that God is never adequately or completely seen. As Samuel Terrien elucidates this point,
'Either there is too much light, in which case the storytellers emphasize the blinding quality of the experience, or there is too little light—the experience occurs in the gloom of night or in a cloud of total darkness—and the storytellers pile up synonyms for obscurity in order to stress divine invisibility.'[2]

Thus, for example, in the previously noted divine 'vision' of Ezekiel, the prophet describes the Lord's appearance (Ezek. 1.28b) 'like the appearance of fire enclosed round about; and downward from what had the appearance of his loins I saw as it were the appearance of fire, and there was brightness round about him. Like the appearance of the bow that is in the cloud on the day of rain, so was the appearance of the brightness round him' (Ezek. 1.27-28a). This is a description the prophet himself calls 'the likeness of the glory of the Lord' (Ezek. 1.28b) more than it is a vision of God.

Third, a true vision of God is something both exceptional and dangerous in the Hebrew Scriptures.[3] Thus, when Moses realized that the Lord God was revealing self in the burning bush, 'Moses hid his face, for he was afraid to look at God' (Exod. 3.6). Later in Exodus God announced to Moses that, though God will 'make all my goodness pass before you ... you cannot see my face; for man shall not see me and live' (Exod. 33.19-20). While it is true that in some cultic contexts, 'to see Yahweh' often had the positive meaning of experiencing the presence of God in the Temple (for example, Pss. 42.3; 84.8; Isa. 38.11), in other contexts, such as Exodus 33, it could be life-threatening. When Isaiah saw Yahweh in the Temple he feared for his life (Isa. 6.5) and when Amos saw the Lord in his fifth vision (Amos 9.1) destruction and death ensued.[4]

Closely related to this pattern in which auditory imagery prevails over visual imagery in divine manifestation is the ban against visual depictions of God at the heart of Israel's law (Exod. 20.4; Deut. 5.8). The aniconic tradition in Israel is not only ancient, but also without a real parallel in the ancient Near East.[5] While it

---

[1] Gerhard Kittel, 'ákoúw', *TDNT* 1:218.
[2] Samuel Terrien, *The Elusive Presence*, Religious Perspectives 26 (Harper & Row, San Francisco, 1978), p.69.
[3] Kittel, *TDNT* 1:218.
[4]. Michael Barré, 'Amos' in *NJBC* 13.23.
[5] Terrien, p.163.

is true that a variety of graphic designs, images and decorations did grace various Jewish buildings[1], 'no certain image of Yahweh has so far been found at any Israelite site.'[2]

The one great exception to these generalizations about visions of God comes from Exod. 24.9-11. In this unusual passage, God was seen directly by humans who actually ate and drank with God: 'And they saw the God of Israel; and there was under his feet as it were a pavement of sapphire stone like the very heaven for clearness. And he did not lay his hand on the chief men of the people of Israel; they beheld God, and ate and drank.' As if to emphasize the point, the passage twice reports that Moses and his companions saw God. Terrien suggests that this story is 'without parallel in the Hebrew tradition' and was shocking to Hellenistic Jews who added the phrase 'God is not seen, only the place where he stood' to verse 10 of this chapter.[3] While this text is extreme it does represent a pattern in stories of divine revelation that emerged from the southern tradition—although it is not clear that the story of Exod. 24.9-11 itself had such an origin. This pattern, as Terrien describes it, is one in which southern theologians increasingly interpreted divine presence and divine revelation through the theologoumenon of the glory.[4] This pattern, however, is a latter development in the history of ancient Israel, while the emphasis on the preparatory, obscuring and dangerous nature of visual encounters with the divine seems to be older and foundational.[5]

2). *The Importance of the organs for hearing and speaking:* Another indicator of concealed oralism in the Old Testament is the importance that this collection of writings gives to the organs for hearing and speaking. There are three different ways in which the Old Testament stresses the organs for hearing and speaking.

First, these scriptures emphasize that the ear and hearing are constitutive for an authentic definition of personhood. While the Hebrew Scriptures refer to the ear as a physical attribute of humans, the text's figurative references to the ear 'as a symbol of the complete process of hearing and, by extension, of understanding and obedience is far more significant.'[6] An introduction to the role of the ear and hearing in the Hebrew Scriptures is provided by Eliphaz who articulates how,

---

[1] See, for example, Joseph Gutmann, *No Graven Images: Studies in Art and the Hebrew Bible* (Ktav, New York, 1970).

[2] Richard Clifford, 'Exodus' in *NJBC* 3.33.

[3] Terrien, p.135.

[4] Terrien, pp.136-138.

[5] Some have also suggested that there was an ancient stratum in Israel's history that put emphasis on vision rather than hearing in divine revelation. As Sanders, for example, notes, 'Anciently a prophet was called a "seer" (1 Sam. 9.9). The emphasis on word rather than vision may be connected with the Hebrew rejection of Idolatry and, indeed, mistrust of any visual aids to religious faith such as are found in most religions, including Christianity itself.' (J. N. Sanders, 'Word' in *IDB* 4:869).

[6] R. C. Denta, 'Ear' in *IDB* 2:1.

starting from the ear, the whole person is activated (Job 4.12-14).[1] To 'open someone's ears' (Isa. 48.8) or to awaken someone's ears (Isa. 50.4) are basic expressions for communicating with another. Other texts from the First Testament suggest that hearing determines one's behaviour and state of being generally (for example, Gen. 3.8-10). It is an organ not simply for acquiring auditory information, but for understanding and receptivity. In some instances the ear serves as a parallel for the heart (Prov. 2.2; 18.15; 23.12), which is the seat of the whole inner life.[2] Thus, Solomon asks for a heart that *hears* so that he might be able to discern between good and evil (1 Kgs. 3.10). In this instance the ear becomes the fundamental metaphor for Solomon's wisdom.[3] These and other examples demonstrate that hearing is constitutive of the whole, developed individual.[4]

Second, the Old Testament emphasizes that the ear and hearing are essential for an authentic relationship with God. Besides serving as a critical means for achieving personhood, the scriptures emphasize that the ear and hearing provide a fundamental link between humans and God. In ancient Israel God was more often heard than seen. Besides the simple quantity or dominance of such such passages, the Hebrew Scriptures further demonstrate that hearing provides an essential link between God and humanity. Without the capacity to hear—literally and metaphorically—humankind would be severely disabled in its ability to sustain a relationship with the God of Israel. The Hebrew Bible stresses that, from the beginning, God has initiated the dialogue: be that at the mythic beginning of time (Gen. 1.26-30), the beginning of the covenant with Abraham (Gen. 12.1-3), or when Yahweh took charge of the existence of Israel (Exod. 23.22).[5] Not only does God speak, but God speaks a law that humans are called to hear and obey. The biblical expression for obeying is to 'listen to' God, to God's voice (Gen. 3.17; 28.7). Similarly to obey God (Isa. 42.24) or to obey God's law (Jer. 9.12) requires first that one hear God[6], and then act. Since God has created the ear (Prov. 20.12) humans have a great responsibility to use their ears wisely, allowing God to open them so that life can be aligned with reality.[7] This point is dramatically made in the daily confession known as the *shema* (Deut. 6.4-9; 11.13-21; Num. 15.37-41), which begins 'Hear, O Israel'. Thus Kittel concludes that an essential feature of biblical religion is that,

'It is a religion of the Word, because it is a religion of action, of obedience to the Word. The prophet is the bearer of the Word of Yahweh which demands obedience and fulfillment. Man is not righteous as he seeks to

---

[1] Thus Wolff concludes, 'Just as the auditory reception of the word by the wise man through the ear changes the whole state of the body, so the hearing determines a man's behaviour and state of health generally.' Hans Walter Wolff, *Anthropology of the Old Testament*, trans. Margaret Kohl (Fortress Press, Philadelphia, 1974), p.76.

[2] *Encyclopedic Dictionary of the Bible*, ed Louis Hartmann (McGraw-Hill, New York, 1963), s.v. 'ear' and 'heart'.

[3] Wolff, p.76.

[4] G. von Rad, *Weisheit*, p.309 as cited in Wolff, p.76.

[5] Xavier Léon-Dufour, *Dictionary of Biblical Theology*, 2nd. ed. (Seabury Press, New York, 1973), s.v. 'communion'.

[6] *Encyclopedic Dictionary of the Bible*, s.v. 'ear'.

[7] K. H. Maahs, 'Ear', in *The International Standard Bible Encyclopedia*, ed. Geoffrey Bromiley, 4 vols. (Eerdmans, Grand Rapids, 1982), 2:2.

apprehend or perceive God by way of thought and vision, but as he hears the command of God and studies to observe it.'[1]

More than any other sense perception, hearing provides the vital link between the God of Israel and humankind.

A third indicator of concealed oralism in the Old Testament is the extended vocabulary employed in the Hebrew scriptures for the organs of speech. Since the received word is incomplete without a response,[2] and the organs of speech articulate that response, so does the First Testament give these organ special attention. 'Whereas the ear and the eye only have one word each in the Old Testament, a whole collection of parts of the body represent the instrument of speech.'[3] The mouth (*peh*) is the main organ of speech mentioned in the Hebrew Scriptures. As the organ that expresses what the ear and eye has perceived, it distinguishes humans from all other creatures and stands quite near to humankind's essential being.[4] Besides the mouth, however, the Hebrew Scriptures also admit a host of other parts of the body that represent the instrument of speechs[1]: *śapā* which literally means lips (Ps. 22.8), but also is a metaphor for language (Isa. 6.7); *lāśōn* is the tongue (Lam. 4.4), but also is a figure for true (2 Sam. 23.2) or false (Ps. 12.3) speech; *ḥek* or palate is literally the seat of the sense of taste (Ps. 119.103); *gārōn* is at once the throat (Jer. 2.25), but also an organ of speech (Isa. 58.1)

3). *The dynamic nature of the Hebrew language and Hebrew thought:* A third indicator of concealed oralism in the Old Testament is what Boman calls the dynamic nature of the Hebrew language and thought. This dynamism is demonstrated by the dynamic character of Hebrew verbs of inaction. According to Boman, Hebrew verbs always tend to express movement or activity.[6] This tendency toward movement or activity is most striking in verbs of inaction such as standing (*natsabh*), sitting (*vashabh*), or stretch out (*shakhabh*). While indicating a position of repose or inactivity, in the Hebrew mind such experiences of stasis were related to the motion that preceded them. Boman concludes that 'motionless and fixed being is for the Hebrews a nonentity; it does not exist for them.'[7] Boman draws a similar conclusion about verbs of condition and quality such as to be/become angry (*'aneph*), or to be/become bright (*'ōr*)[8], as well as the verb 'to

---

[1] Kittel, 'ákoúo', *TDNT* 1:218.

[2] 'According to the Hebraic meaning of the word *truth*, to listen, to receive the word of God, is not only to lend it an attentive ear but also to open one's heart to it; it is to be put into practice, that is, to obey.' (Léon-Dufour, s.v. 'listen').

[3] Wolff, p.77.

[4] K. H. Maahs, 'Mouth' *The International Standard Bible Encyclopedia*, 2:428.

[5] Much of what follows comes from Wolff, pp.77-78.

[6] Thorlief Boman, *Hebrew Thought Compared with Greek*, trans. Jules Moreau (Westminster Press, Philadelphia, 1960), pp.28-31.

[7] *Ibid.*, p.31.

[8] *Ibid.*, pp.31-35.

be' (hayah).[1] Tresmontant concurs when considering the nature of understanding (*bina*) in the prophetic writings. He explains,

'What the prophets call understanding, *bina*, is not a faculty, an *organon* endowed with certain *a priori* categories, a power that would pass into action under certain circumstances. Understanding *is* action, the act of intellection of subsistent truth. Hebrew, a concrete language, never speaks of understanding except in such a context of truth's fruition.'[2]

Boman concludes that, for the Hebrews, the world itself possessed an active character, and was always in motion.[3]

ORALITY IN EMERGING CHRISTIANITY

The Hellenistic Context: Almost four centuries before the birth of Christ, Alexander the Great (d. 323 BCE) conquered the whole of the eastern Mediterranean world. Besides conquering nations, Alexander also transformed the Near East by imposing his own culture and language upon the peoples he subdued throughout the Mediterranean. Although his empire was divided among his generals after his death, the influence of Alexander's Hellenizing campaign continued for centuries. This was true even in Palestine where the Jews did not reestablish their political independence until almost 150 years after the death of Alexander. Although they attempted to assert their cultural independence from Hellenism as well, this effort was short lived and ultimately unsuccessful. Rome conquered the Jewish monarchy in 63 BCE and continued the process of Hellenization. Thus it was in a Jewish milieu under the political and cultural influence of the Greco-Roman world that Christianity emerged.

The culture that Alexander exported from Greece was one in which seeing rather than hearing was celebrated as the most important human sense. This development occurred between the time of Homer (before 700 BCE) and Plato (d. 347 BCE). Although Greek culture at the time of Homer was not without writing, and at the time of Plato was not without epic poetry or oral performance, in the latter period the emphasis was clearly shifting from the ear to the eye. It was not Plato who initiated this change. In his writings there is a general absence of argument on the subject and he simply seems to take for granted the pre-eminence of vision.[4] Plato does, however, become the great prophet of visualiza-

---

[1] *Ibid.*, pp.38-49.

[2] Claude Tresmontant, *A Study of Hebrew Thought*, trans. Michael Francis Gibson (Desclee Company, New York, 1960), p.125.

[3] Boman, pp.49-51; Boman's discussion of the dynamism of Hebrew thought contrasted with Greek thought needs to be read with caution. As will be demonstrated, Greek thought before Plato (d. 347 BCE) was also dynamic; and Hebrew thought after the influence of Alexander the Great demonstrates certain Hellenized influences. Thus, Boman's analysis of what we have called hidden oralisms in the Hebrew Scriptures is especially demonstrative of a type of thinking prominent before the exile.

[4] Evelyn Fox Keller and Christine R. Grontkowski, 'The Mind's Eye' in *Discovering Reality*, ed. Sandra Harding and Merrill Hintikka (D. Reidel Publishing, Dordrecht-Boston-London, 1983), p.209.

tion[1] and after him there is little doubt that vision is held to be the most excellent of the senses. The influence of Plato and the philosophy that emerged from a society that valued seeing over hearing was extensive and pervasive. Ultimately it provided a framework for Western civilization that would allow one to assert that seeing is believing.

Despite this powerful Hellenistic influence, the ancient world in general—and Palestine in particular—were places in which hearing continued to dominate. Although segments of the culture communicated significantly through literary means[2], the culture of late Western antiquity was what Paul Achtemeier calls 'a culture of high residual orality.'[3] One irrefutable symbol of this residual orality was the continued practice of reading aloud. 'The oral environment was so pervasive that no writing occurred that was not vocalized . . . even solitary readers, reading only to themselves, read aloud.'[4] Thus it appears that the Hellenized world that provided the context for the emergence of Christianity, maintained a distinctive auditory environment in which orality was highly valued.

Hellenized Judaism, in particular, continued as a culture with high residual orality. While there are many symbols of the continued emphasis on orality in Hellenistic Judaism around the time of Christ, one of the most important of these is the growing importance during this period of the oral Torah (*Torah she-b'a peh*). The Pharisees were a small group within Palestinian Judaism that emerged during the period of the second Temple. They distinguished themselves from other Jews by claiming that,

'when God revealed the Torah to Moses at Mount Sinai, God gave the Torah in two parts. One part was in writing . . . the other part was not written down, but was meant to be handed on through memorization and repetition of the precise language that had been memorized from one generation

---

[1] Eric Havelock, *Preface to Plato: A History of the Greek Mind* (Belknap Press of Harvard University Press, Cambridge MA, 1963), p.vii. Also Keller and Grontkowski who comment, 'So evident was it to him [Plato] that vision enjoys an elevated status over the other senses that he was able merely to assert its pre-eminence, at least implicitly, without feeling it necessary to argue the point. In his only extensive analysis of the senses *per se*, he entirely separates the discussion of vision from the discussion of the other four senses [*Timaeus*, 61d-68e]. He describes the creation of the sense of sight in the same context as the creation of soul and intelligence in human beings; all of the other senses are described in the context of the creation of man's material nature. He also says, in *Timaeus*, that "the first organs they (the gods) fashioned were those that gave us light" [45b]. He comments elsewhere on the intrinsic nobility of this construction, as for example, in *Phaedrus*, when referring to "the keenest of all the senses" [250d] and in the Republic when he observes: "Have you noticed how extremely lavish the designer of our senses was when he gave us the faculty of sight?" [507c]' p.210.

[2] Pliny the elder, for example, speaking about the history of paper, noted how a shortage of paper could completely upset life in the Roman Empire. *Natural History* XIII.27.89, as edited by H. Rackham in 10 volumes, Loeb Classical Library (Harvard University Press, Cambridge MA, 1945), 370:153.

[3] Paul Achtemeier, '*Omne Verbum Sonat:* The New Testament and the Oral Environment of Late Western Antiquity' in *Journal of Biblical Literature* 109 (1990) p.12.

[4] Achtemeier, pp.15-16.

to the next. This other half of the Torah is called, therefore, the Oral Torah, or the Torah which is memorized.'[1]

Between ca. 200 BCE and 100 CE the Pharisees strongly asserted their right to rule all the Jews by virtue of their possession of this Oral Torah.[2] Eventually the Pharisees succeeded in wresting spiritual leadership in Palestinian Judaism away from the Sadducees who did not believe in these claims about the oral Torah. The Pharisees' growing influence, with its reassertion of the oral component of the law, effectively underscores the sensitive auditory environment of first century Palestinian Judaism, and its continued emphasis on orality.

The Jesus Experience: Just as one can not consider the oral nature of emerging Judaism apart from its cultural context, so one cannot understand the auditory aspects of the Jesus experience apart from Palestinian Judaism at the beginning of the Common Era. Jesus was a Jew and was part of a culture and religious tradition that valued hearing as much if not more than seeing—especially in the transmission of religious truths. This auditory awareness, common to all Palestinian Jews of the period, seems to have been especially true for Jesus because of particular geographic and linguistic circumstances. Greek was the language that, more than any other in the Ancient Near East, served as a vehicle for the ascendancy of sight over sound in Western thought. One can surmise, however, that because Jesus was a Jew from rural Palestine who only spoke Aramaic, the Hellenistic tendency to prize the visual over the auditory was significantly muted.

We have already noted how teaching in Judaism was essentially an oral enterprise.[3] As a teacher, Jesus was inevitably engaged in this auditory venture. While it is true that some rabbis did employ writing as a way to communicate their teachings, there is no evidence that Jesus ever did so, even though he could read (Luke 4.16ff) and write (John 8.6). Jesus' reliance on oral instead of written communication may have been a conscious choice. The basis for any such choice would have been an awareness of oral communication's 'greater power for reaching and transforming the people of the day.'[4]

Was Jesus unique in this regard, or could his preaching style simply be understood to be similar to that other rabbis of his day?[5] The latter position would seem to ignore a radical difference between the speech of Jesus and that of other Jewish teachers—a difference that has its own theological significance.[6] In

---

[1] Jacob Neusner, *The Way of Torah*, 3rd ed. (Duxbury Press, North Scituate MA, 1979), p.13; also, his *The Memorized Torah: The Mnemonic System of the Mishnah* (Scholars Press, Chico CA, 1985).

[2] Jacob Neusner, *From Politics to Piety: The Emergence of Pharisaic Judaism* (Ktav Publishing House, New York, 1979), p.11.

[3] de Vaux, *Ancient Israel* 1:49.

[4] Harold Coward, *Sacred Word and Sacred Text: Scripture in World Religions* (Orbis Books, Maryknoll NY, 1988), p.36.

[5] For such a perspective, see Birger Gerhardsson, *The Origins of the Gospel Traditions* (Fortress Press, Philadelphia, 1979).

[6] Amos Wilder, *Early Christian Rhetoric: The Language of the Gospel* (Harvard University Press, Cambridge MA, 1971), p.15.

outlining this difference, Amos Wilder emphasizes the extemporaneous nature of Jesus' speech: not carefully crafted or methodically thought out beforehand, but ingeniously improvised in a specific context. According to Wilder, Jesus' speech was naïve, not studied: 'It is *extempore* and directed to the occasion, it is not calculated to serve some future hour. This utterance is dynamic, actual, immediate, reckless of posterity; not coded for catechesis or repetition.'[1]

If Wilder's analysis is accurate then Jesus, unlike other rabbis of first century Palestine, 'was not schooling his followers in a learned mode that could be passed on to future generations. Rather, he spoke to the immediate crisis of the day in a free and spontaneous style.'[2] And it was a particular crisis of his day that demanded this new style of speech-act.[3]

As an eschatological prophet[4], Jesus was aware that the kingdom was in the process of being revealed.[5] While there were those in Palestinian Judaism whose primary expressions of eschatological hope were written, 'there was another stratum of society whose hopes were expressed in a more "activist," even "revolutionary" manner.'[6] Jesus' eschatological message, understood in this context, was a dynamic and revolutionary speech-act that eschewed writing. 'The act of writing presupposes continuities and a future . . . but for Jesus and his generation, history was fractured, time's course was in dissolution, continuities were broken. Jesus' word was for the present, the last hour.'[7] Thus his examples are realistic and vivid—deftly chosen from existential experience.[8] This immediacy of language well serves the eschatological message in a style that is unique and memorable. As Wilder summarizes,

'The incomparable felicity and patterning of his sayings is indeed evident, but this formal perfection is not a matter of mnemonics; it is the countersign of the most effective communication of the moment. Naturally his words and parables were remembered and retold, often with great accuracy, so lucid and inevitable was his phrasing. But here as always the new speech of the Gospel was not a matter of words on a table but a word in the heart, not a copybook for recitation but winged words for life'.[9]

Jesus the rabbi embodied the Jewish predilection for orality over visualization: the speech-act over writing. As an eschatological prophet, he not only relied upon a heightened auditory environment, but transformed it through

---

[1] Wilder, p.13.
[2] Coward, p.37.
[3] Wilder, p.4.
[4] See, for example, E. P. Sanders, *Jesus and Judaism* (Fortress Press, Philadelphia, 1985), p.8 and *passim*.
[5] Joachim Jeremias, *The Parables of Jesus*, rev. ed. (Charles Scribner's Sons, New York, 1963); for a summary and critique of Jeremias' position, see Norman Perrin, *Jesus and the Language of the Kingdom* (Fortress Press, Philadelphia, 1976), pp.91-107.
[6] Adela Yarbro Collins, 'Eschatology and Apocalypticism' in *NJBC* 81:41.
[7] Wilder, p.14.
[8] C. H. Dodd, *The Parables of the Kingdom*, rev. ed. (Scribner's, New York, 1961), pp.9-10.
[9] Wilder, p.15.

revolutionary forms of speech that could not be contained by writing. And, as the word made flesh, he proclaimed and embodied the word so uniquely that the kingdom was revealed in a singular and unrepeatable articulation.

The Oral Kerygma: Jesus' revolutionary style of preaching evoked a similar revolution in the language of his disciples. Although the early community was concerned to hand on Jesus' teaching, they did not persuade people to believe in Jesus by repeating his teachings (*didaché*), but through preaching (*kerygma*)—an act that had more in common with town criers or auctioneers than traditionally understood rabbinic discourse.[1] 'Although Christianity from the very beginning had a scripture, the Hebrew Scriptures, the faith of the earliest Christians was evoked by and focused on a person, Jesus of Nazareth. Jesus, in the earliest Christian communities, was known not in bible texts but in missionary preaching, oral tradition and charismatic experience.'[2]

It is from this perspective that Ernst Fuchs can suggest that primitive Christianity itself was a speech-phenomenon[3] that did not first concern itself with written forms. Rather, in the memory and example of Jesus, the first disciples went about proclaiming the good news, and in so doing contributed to a heightened auditory environment in which Jesus was proclaimed. It is this oral performance that lay at the heart of the early Christian message, and generated the new religious form of truth known as the gospel. It was only through this auditory kerygma—what Frederick Crowe calls 'gospelling the gospel'[4]—that belief was possible.[5]

Residual Orality in the New Testament: With increasing frequency scholars are approaching the New Testament not simply as a collection of literary works but as attempts by various communities to translate into writing what was essentially an auditory phenomenon. The gospel of Mark, for example, is dominated by the oral form of storytelling.[6] Not only the gospel of Mark, however, but all of the New Testament documents 'are oral to the core, both in their creation and in their performance.'[7] Rooted in the free oral dialogue of Jesus and his disciples, that was memorized and repeated for believers, the stories and parables were eventually written down.

'But even when the face-to-face rhetorical forms of the beginnings gave way to the conventionality of written records and letters, these are still characterized by a perennially dramatic element which goes back to the very nature of the Christian religion. The Christian styles tend to evoke or restore the face-to-face encounter.'[8]

---

[1] C. H. Dodd, *The Apostolic Preaching and Its Developments* (Baker Book House, Grand Rapids MI, 1980), pp.7-8.

[2] Coward, p.34.

[3] 'Die Sprache im Neuen Testament', *Zur Frage nach dem historischen Jesus* (Tübingen, 1960), p.261, as cited and translated by Wilder, p.10.

[4] Frederick Crowe, *Theology of the Christian Word* (Paulist, New York, 1978), p.35.

[5] Gerhard Friedrich, '*kerygma*' in *TDNT* 3:716.

[6] Kelber, especially pp.44-89.

[7] Achtemeier, p.19.

[8] Wilder, p.16.

Like the Hebrew scriptures, the New Testament preserves many traces of residual orality. This 'concealed oralism' is much more prominent in the New Testament than in the Hebrew scriptures as the time between the oral event and written form for the former is far more condensed than that same process for the latter. While there are a number of indicators of the New Testament's concealed orality, a brief consideration of three of them should make the point.

First is the emblematic role of parables in the New Testament. As Schillebeeckx and others have noted, Jesus not only taught in parables but himself was a parable.[1] As Jesus announced the kingdom, so were his parables intimately wed to that announcement.[2] Parables were certainly one of the most characteristic story forms employed by Jesus. Kelber reminds us that the 'oral propriety of parabolic stories requires little argument.'[3] Parables are oral forms that presume and require the speech-event for their power. Even when they are translated into written forms, they retain various oral characteristics. One of these is the presence of certain mnemonic devices.[4] In the Gospel of Mark, for example, both the parable of the sower and that of the mustard seed employ the mnemonic device of contrast, which renders these stories 'orally impressionable'.[5] Paul Ricoeur has suggested that another characteristic of many parables is what he terms *extravagance*.[6] According to Kelber, this concept of extravagance further illuminates the mnemonic process of parables. As he explains, 'Over and above the mnemonic patterning, it is the element of excess and irregularity that eases remembering. The trivial facilitates identification, but oddness makes these stories memorable. For one what remembers is not the pane in the window, but the crack in the pane.'[7]

The residual orality of the New Testament is also demonstrated by the dominance of auditory over visual imagery for revelation and faith. Although the verbs of seeing outnumber the verbs of hearing in the New Testament, this

---

[1] Edward Schillebeeckx, *Jesus*, trans. Hubert Hoskins (Vintage Books, New York, 1981), p.155.

[2] Dominic Crossan, *The Dark Interval* (Argus Publications, Niles IL, 1975), p.124.

[3] Kelber, p.58; much of what follows is reliant upon Kelber, pp.57-64.

[4] Such as alliteration, paranomasia, appositional equivalence, proverbial and aphoristic diction, contrasts and antitheses, synonymous, antithetical, synthetic and tautologic parallelism, etc. (Kelber, p.27). For a further discussion of mnemonic devices in oral speech, see Marcel Jousse, *Études de Psychologie Linguistique: Le Style Oral Rhythmique et Mnémontechnique chez les Verbo-Moteurs* (Gabriel Beauchesne, Paris, 1925).

[5] Kelber notes that the display of opposites appeals to the imagination and holds the attention as do few rhetorical devices. p.59.

[6] Paul Ricoeur, 'Biblical Hermeneutics' in *Semeia* 4 (1975) 32; Dominic Crossan calls this an 'antitraditional' story element, in *In Parables: The Challenge of the Historical Jesus* (Harper & Row, New York, 1973), p.118; Robert Funk calls it 'the imaginative shock' in the story, in *Language, Hermeneutic, and the Word of God: The Problem of Language in the New Testament and Contemporary Theology* (Harper & Row, New York, 1966), p.193; Wilder calls it the 'trait of hyperbole' in these stories, in *The Language of the Gospel*, p.85.

[7] Kelber, p.61.

does not mean that seeing is the more important of the senses. It is true that at some moments seeing is more highly esteemed than hearing (John 8.38) in the redemptive enterprise. The sense of sight takes on particular significance in the gospel of John.[1] In general, however, the visual does not replace the auditory in the New Testament at moments of revelation or faith, where 'there can be no doubt as to the primacy of hearing.'[2] Even when the New Testament depicts revelatory events in visual terms, such events usually acquire their true significance through what is heard. For example, the appearance of the angel acquires its true significance through the accompanying message at the annunciation (Luke 1.28-37); the baptism of Jesus acquires its true significance with the voice after Jesus' baptism (Mark 1.11); and, the transfiguration acquires its true significance with the revelatory word (Matt. 17.5). As Amos Wilder summarizes,

> 'The New Testament speaks of the divine apprehension in terms of all the senses, not only hearing and sight but touch and smell (the last in the form of incense and fragrant odours). Yet the hearing mode is primary. The spirit may be rapt in vision, but it is with the heart that man hears the word of faith and with his mouth that he confesses and is saved (Rom 10.8-10). Language, then, is more fundamental than graphic representation, except where the latter is itself a transcript in some sense of the word of God.'[3]

A further testimony to the oral genesis and foundation of the New Testament is the existence of numerous parallel passages that are yet markedly different from each other. No example of this is more striking than that of the institution narratives.[4] While there is a core of material that is common to the four institution narratives recorded in the New Testament—both in structure[5] and in text[6]—there is yet enormous diversity between these citations.[7] This diversity can best be explained by what Jeremias calls 'a living process of growth in the tradition.'[8] At the basis of these varying texts was an historical, oral event. This event, in turn, served as the basis for the liturgical practice of emerging Christianity. It was the liturgical context—the cultic speech-event of emerging Christianity—that gave rise to the parallel yet diverse institution accounts imbedded in the New Testament. The institution narratives are one example of residual orality, in which oral transmission and enactment generated written texts. The residual orality of the institution narrative continues to be affirmed by various segments of Christianity which over the centuries have employed variations on the biblical texts in ritual enactment.[9]

---

[1] Wilhelm Michaelis, 'orao' in *TDNT* 5:361-364.

[2] Michaelis, 'orao' in *TDNT* 5:348.

[3] Wilder, p.11.

[4] 1 Cor. 11.23-25; Mark 14.22-24; Matt. 26.26-27; Luke 22.19-20; while not a parallel passage, an independent version of Jesus' word of interpretation over the bread can be found in John 6.21c.

[5] See Gregory Dix, *The Shape of the Liturgy*, 2nd ed. (Dacre Press, London, 1975 [1945]), pp.48-50.

[6] Joachim Jeremias, *The Eucharistic Words of Jesus*, trans. Norman Perrin (Fortress, Philadelphia, 1977), pp.189-196.

[7] Jeremias, pp.160-173.

[8] Jeremias, p.105.

[9] The current official text of the Latin Rite of the Roman Catholic Church, for example, is a variation on various biblical texts.

SUMMARY

This brief introduction to the dominance of auditory over visual imagery in divine manifestations, the importance of the organs for hearing and speaking and the dynamic nature of the Hebrew language and Hebrew thought as revealed through the Old Testament suggests that, despite the fact that writing might have been widespread in ancient Israel, there continued what might be called an 'auditory bias' in Israel. This observation finds a corollary in the work of Jack Goody who asserts that 'the division between "literacy" and "orality" is never a question of crossing a single frontier, a simple binary shift.'[1] Rather, as Goody notes, even literary composition requires oral or sub-oral processes. Thus, while the Old Testament was redacted by a society at least at the stage of craft-literacy, the texts exhibit the kind of concealed oralism which allows us to assert the auditory bias of Hebrew life and thought.

At the dawn of Christianity, this heightened auditory environment endured, despite Hellenizing influences that valued seeing over hearing. For Jesus, in particular, the spontaneous word-event was a fundamental characteristic of his ministry. Announcing the immediacy of the good news in a manner 'reckless of posterity'[2] typified his public ministry, and that of his followers. Despite the emergence of written forms like the Gospel, a primacy of audition continued to characterize developing Christianity. For them, hearing was believing.

There have been few explicit references to music in this chapter, much less the music of ancient Christianity, which is the prime concern of this monograph. Before explicitly addressing the topic of music, however, some acknowledgement and understanding of the broader sonic environment of the ancient Near East, Judaism and emerging Christianity is essential. As has been noted before, and will be noted again, twentieth century Western concepts of music do not necessarily provide an adequate framework for understanding what another culture or another time might consider music or musical. This is especially true when people from a visually dominated tradition attempt to raise musical questions about an oral society. Appreciating something of the nature of an auditory environment in general, and the auditory environment of the movement or culture under investigation in particular, are first steps in gaining such understanding.

---

[1] Goody, p.106.
[2] Wilder, p.13.

2. The Temple of Herod

Following the instruction of his father, King David (d. ca. 962 BCE), Solomon (d. ca. 922 BCE) built the first Temple in Jerusalem (1 Chron. 22.6-8). It was a small[1] but sumptuous structure, which took almost seven years to complete (1 Kgs. 6.37-38).[2] This Temple soon became the national religious centre of Israel, overshadowing every other sanctuary in the country.[3] Destroyed by the invading Babylonians in 587 BCE, the Temple was rebuilt according to a more modest plan after the period of captivity in about 515 BCE (Ezra 5.16; Hag. 2.3). Ravaged by time and wars, this structure was in considerable disrepair by the first century BCE. Herod the Great (d. 4 BCE) demolished this second Temple and began building a magnificent replacement in about the year 20 BCE. This building, completed by 64 AD, was destroyed in 70 AD during the revolt against the Romans.

The new Temple, like the two before it, sat high on a hill overlooking the Kidron valley. The Temple proper in this new complex was about the same size as Solomon's building. It seemed more magnificent, however, because Herod doubled the size of the Temple mount and constructed a far more extensive enclosure wall.[4] Within this impressive enclosed setting were a further series of walls and courtyards. Moving from the outermost to the innermost, these were (1) the Court of the Gentiles, open to all; (2) the court of the Women, open to all Jews; (3) the court of Israel[5], open only to Jewish men; and (4) the Court of the Priests, open only to the priests. The altar for the daily sacrifices stood within the Court of Israel. Although sacrifices had once been offered in many different sanctuaries throughout Israel[6], the Temple in Jerusalem came to be the only

---

[1] measuring approximately 105 feet long and 30 feet wide. John Castelot, 'Religious Institutions of Israel' in *NJBC* 76:43.

[2] On the architecture of Solomon's Temple, see Jean Ouelette, 'The Solomonic Dᵉbîr according to the Hebrew Text of 1 Kings 6', *Journal of Biblical Literature* 89 (1970) 338-343.

[3] e.g. Beersheba (Gen. 26.25), Bethel (Gen.1 12.8), Dan (Judg. 18.29-31), Gilgal (Josh. 4.19-20), Mamre (Gen. 13.18), Mizpah (Judg. 20.1), Ophrah (Judg. 6.11f), Shechem (Gen.12.6-7), and Shiloh (Josh. 18.1).

[4] Robert North, 'Biblical Archaeology' in *NJBC* 74:138.

[5] According to the Mishnah, Temple musicians stood on a platform that divided the Court of Priests from the Court of Israel. *Middoth* 2.6. Bathja Bayer's comments about the value of the Mishnah in reconstructing Temple worship are worth repeating: 'Much of the mishnaic narrative concerning music in the Temple service is based on eyewitness memories. The information is often very precise, such as the description of the daily morning sacrifice in Mishnah *Tamid* and the numbers of instruments in the Temple orchestra in Mishnah *Arakhin*. The figure of the Temple Musician appears much more clearly.' (Bathja Bayer, 'Music' in *EJ* 12:566).

[6] see n. 3 above; sacrifices were also offered at Beersheba (Gen. 46.1), Bethshemesh (1 Sam. 6.15), Hebron (2 Sam. 15.12), Shiloh (1 Sam. 1.4), etc.

FIGURE 1. HEROD'S TEMPLE
Plan of Herod's Temple (after Vincent-Steve as cited in Norman Perrin and
Dennis C. Dulling, *The New Testament: An Introduction*, 2nd ed. (Hartcourt,
Brace, Jovanovich, New York, 1982), p.xx.

place of sacrifice for the Jews, except for Samaritans who offered sacrifice on Mount Gerizim.[1] For all practical purposes, the destruction of the Jerusalem Temple in 70 CE marked the end of Jewish sacrifice.

TEMPLE MUSICIANS

King David is remembered as having established professional Temple music (1 Chron. 15), and having placed Levites in charge (1 Chron. 25). The earliest accounts of the Temple (2 Sam. 6), however, do not mention professional Temple musicians, which may have been a post-Davidic development.[2] The pre-exilic material in the Hebrew scriptures give little evidence for Temple singers. However, information about other sanctuaries of the same period, both inside and outside of Palestine, lead scholars like de Vaux to conclude that the first Temple retained the services of professional musicians.[3] The role of prophets in the musical life of Israel or the First Temple has never been clear. As Werner notes, they have sometimes been considered priestly Temple singers, or non-priestly singers attached to the Temple, or even independent singers sharply distinct from the musical hierarchy of the official cult.[4] Whatever their role, they were eventually eclipsed by the Levitical musicians. The earliest evidence indicates that Levitical musicians needed to be at least 30 years of age in order to serve in the Temple[5], although this age limits fluctuated[6], possibly because of an increased demand for Levites in the service of the Temple.[7] One source indicates that Levites served only until they were 50 years of age (Num. 4.3).

According to the Chronicler, two hundred and eighty-eight musicians were appointed to serve in the Temple (1 Chron. 25.7). While this may simply be a mythic number born of the Chronicler's fertile imagination, its historicity—especially for the post-exilic Temple—cannot be completely discounted. The Chronicler notes that priests were divided into twenty-four classes or sections, and that the time of service for each section was determined by casting lots (1 Chron. 24.4-18). The Levites, also divided into twenty-four sections, similarly cast lots in order to determine the sequence of their service (1 Chron. 25.9-31). Each section of priests and Levites served in the Temple for a week at a time,

---

[1] This Temple seems to date, according to archaeological evidence, from early in the Greek Era (333-63 BCE). See, for example, Robert Bull, 'The Excavation of Tell er-Ras on Mt. Gerizim' in *Biblical Archaeologist* 31 (1968) 58-72.

[2] This discrepancy serves as a reminder that, although Chronicles describes practices of the first Temple, the post-exilic composition of Chronicles raises serious questions about the accuracy of much of this information. See the summary by Robert North, 'The Chronicler' in *NJBC* 23:4 & 6.

[3] de Vaux, *Ancient Israel* 2:382; de Vaux also surmises that, since singers 'returned' from exile (Neh. 7.44), these offices must have existed before the Exile, although 'in those days they would not have been Levites'. (2:382).

[4] Eric Werner, 'Jewish Music: Liturgical' in *NGDMM* 9:617.

[5] 1 Chr. 23.3; also Num. 4.3 and 2 Chr. 31.17.

[6] In Num. 8.24 the age requirement for Levitical service is 25, and in Ezra 3.8 and 1 Chron. 23.27 it is lowered to 20 years of age.

[7] Robert North, ' "Kittim" war or "Sectaries" Liturgy?' in *Biblica* 39 (1958) 90.

twice yearly.[1] The Chronicler's calculation of two hundred and eighty-eight musicians allows for the existence of twenty-four sections, each comprised of twelve musicians. Although one cannot project this number into pre-exilic times, it does reinforce the impression that musicians of the first Temple served in groups of singers and/or instrumentalists rather than as individual precentors.[2] The number of musicians who served in the post-exilic Temple was apparently larger than that of the first Temple.[3]

It is quite possible that twelve was the minimum number of musicians required to accompany sacrifices.[4] The Mishnah does make the statement that the minimum number of Levitical musicians is twelve.[5] This number is repeated by various authors, but usually as a specific reference to the number of instrumentalists in the Temple.[6] Idelsohn further suggests that a minimum of 12 singers as well at each Temple service. It is possible, however, that the mishnaic

---

[1] 'Forty-eight weeks of the year were thus distributed between twenty-four divisions; the remaining weeks being festival weeks . . . during which all Israel made pilgrimage to Jerusalem'. (Philip Birnbaum, *Encyclopedia of Jewish Concepts* (Sanhedrin Press, New York, 1979), s.v. 'Ma'amadoth.')

[2] A position made all the more believable when one reckons with the demands of music making in an outdoor setting, as well as the need for this music to accompany [i.e. 'cover the sounds of'] animal sacrifices.

[3] de Vaux, *Ancient Israel* 2:392.

[4] I say minimum because, even if a division of twelve Levites assumed responsibility for Temple music for one week every six months, it is unlikely that they would be sufficiently familiar with the Temple rituals and procedures to execute their duties without the help [and musical support?] of the regular Temple staff, such as the director of music noted in the Mishnah (*Shekalim* 5.1). Joachim Jeremias suggests that there were two permanent Levite musicians in the Temple who oversaw the music and coordinated the groups of Levites taking their turn in service to the Temple. (Joachim Jeremias, *Jerusalem in the Time of Jesus* (Fortress Press, Philadelphia, 1969), pp.173 & 208).

[5] *Arakhin* 2.6.

[6] A. Z. Idelsohn, for example, states 'the total minimum number required for the orchestra was twelve instruments [i.e. a minimum of two lyres (*nēbel*), a minimum of nine harps (*kinnôor*), and one cymbal, to which two *ḥā līl* [flutes] were added on twelve festal days during the year.' (*Jewish Music* (Schocken Books, New York, 1967 [1929]), p.17). Eric Werner also notes that the Temple's orchestra consisted of never less than 12 and rarely more than thirty-six instruments. (Eric Werner, *The Sacred Bridge*, vol. 2 (Ktav, New York, 1984), p.3). Jeremias cites *Arakhin* 2.6 as evidence that there must be no less than twelve singers serving in the Temple at one time (*Jerusalem in the Time of Jesus*, p.208, n. 199).

It is possible to calculate 12 instrumentalists in the Mishnah from a passage in *Arakhin* 2.5, which states 'There were never less than two trumpets, and their number could be increased without end; there were never less than nine lyres, and their number could be increased without end; but of cymbals there was but one.' However, this passage does not reconcile with an earlier section in the same tractate which notes 'They played on never less than two harps or more than six' (*Arakhin* 2.3). Werner does comment that 'the trumpets were never mixed with the rest of the orchestra—being used for signals exclusively.' (*Sacred Bridge* 2:3). Substituting the two 'harps' for the two 'trumpets' would render the number twelve and seem to reconcile these two passages.

passage which Idelsohn relies upon for this conclusion[1] is not referring to singers alone, but to Levites who sing and accompany themselves on lyres and harps.[2]

While a Levite's position was hereditary, the training for Temple musicianship developed beyond familial tutoring. Late rabbinic sources report that the musical training of a Levitical singer took at least five years of intensive preparation.[3] While this suggests a very sophisticated training process, such is not improbable for the post-exilic Temple, given the intricate workings of the Temple as reported by the Chronicler as well as the developed state of professional musicianship in the royal courts and Temples of the ancient Near East.[4] As members of a professional 'singing guild'[5], it is quite probable that the post-exilic Levitical singers underwent lengthy training and apprenticeships, before assuming any regular musical role in Israel's national worship.

In summary, we can say that Temple musicians served in groups not as individuals; there seemed to have been a balance between instruments and voices in the music of the Temple; most of the accompanying instruments were string instruments[6]; the musicians were ordinarily male[7], adults[8], well trained, and (at least in post-exilic times) Levites; the number 12 was an idealized quorum of Temple musicians.

---

[1] *Arakhin* 2.6.

[2] This interpretation is bolstered by the continuation of that passage which allows for male children to join in the music making. The children, however 'did not join in the singing with harp and lyre, but with the mouth alone.' The implication is that the adults, on the other hand, join in the sing with lyre and harp, i.e. accompany themselves on instruments.

[3] B. *Hullin* 24a.

[4] Sendry's suggestion that ancient Israel knew an 'Academy of Music . . . in which hundreds of students were continuously trained for a professional career' is an extreme view and unsupported by the evidence. (Alfred Sendry, *Music in the Social and Religious Life of Antiquity* (Fairleigh Dickson University Press, Rutherford-Madison-Teaneck, 1974), pp.103-4).

[5] H. H. Rowley, *Worship in Ancient Israel: Its Forms and Meaning* (SPCK, London, 1967), p.205.

[6] 'A small male choir (occasionally heightened by boys' descants) accompanied only by the plucked strings of lyres and harps; cymbals, trumpets and horns sounded only between the musical sections marked in the Psalm text with the word *sela*. This reserved character of Hebrew Temple music contrasts sharply with the drumming, rattling, and ecstatic clamour heard in most of the heathen cult rituals.' (Hanoch Avenary, *The New Oxford Companion to Music,* ed. Denis Arnold, 2 vols. (Oxford University Press, Oxford-New York, 1983), s.v. 'Jewish Music').

[7] While women definitely assumed musical roles in the courts of the ancient monarchy, and might have contributed to the music making of the early Temple, their participation 'in the Temple choir is nowhere traceable.' (Idelsohn, *Jewish Music,* p.16). Alfred Sendry offers a different perspective: 'There is no doubt that women, too, participated in the Levitical music, at least in the early period.' (Sendry, *Music in the Social and Religious Life of Antiquity,* p.104).

[8] With boys joining on certain occasions.

It is common to refer to the psalter as the songbook of the Temple. This phrase is as helpful as it is misleading. There is general agreement today—largely because of the work of Sigmund Mowinckel[1]—that, from their inception, the psalms were intimately related to Israel's cult. Such does not mean, however, that all or even most of the psalms were related to Temple worship.[2] Very few of the psalms have specific and identifiable liturgical references that allow them to be linked with any certainty to worship[3] or, more particularly, with worship in the Temple. While the structure and content of some psalms suggests that they were employed in the rituals of the Temple[4], and the Mishnah remembers that certain other psalms were sung on particular days in the Temple[5], all of the psalms were not employed there[1], and other texts besides the psalms were sung in Temple worship.

While it is not possible to identify with certainty these other texts sung in Temple worship, the Old Testament does offer some clues about such texts. As Stuhlmueller notes, ancient Israel undoubtedly possessed collections of sacred melodies that developed at its various shrines as well as various traditional songs that would have been sung at community gatherings.[7] Examples of the latter include the song of Deborah (Judg. 5), the Blessing of Moses (Deut. 33) and the Song of Moses (Deut. 32). Who is to say that such traditional or community songs were not a part of Temple worship?—especially in the early years of the Temple when the songs of the common people rather than those of the professional musicians may have dominated. The Mishnah gives the impression

---

[1] For example, see Sigmund Mowinckel, *The Psalms in Israel's Worship*, 2 vols., trans. D. R. Ap-Thomas (Basil Blackwell, Oxford, 1962).

[2] 'It is possible that fewer psalms were composed directly for the Temple liturgy than we often suppose to have been the case. The Temple, moreover, exercised less direction in the formation of the psalter than we are inclined to think.' (Carroll Stuhlmueller, *Psalms: A Biblical-Theological Commentary*, 2 vols., Old Testament Message 21-22 (Michael Glazier, Wilmington DE, 1983), 1:47).

[3] Ps. 81, for example, seems clearly related to the feast of Tabernacles.

[4] Ps. 15, for example, may have been employed as part of an entrance liturgy in the Temple; Ps. 24 may have accompanied a liturgical procession to the Temple.

[5] 'This was the singing which the Levites used to sing in the Temple. On the first day they sang "The earth is the Lord's and all that therein is, the round world and they that dwell therein" [Ps. 24]; on the second day they sang "Great is the Lord and highly to be praised in the city of our God, even upon his holy hill" [Ps. 48]; on the third day they sang "God standeth in the congregation of God, he is a judge among the gods" [Ps. 82]; on the fourth day they sang "O Lord God to whom vengeance belongeth, thou God to whom vengeance belongeth show thyself" [Ps. 94]; on the fifth day they sang "Sing we merrily unto God our strength, make a cheerful noise unto the God of Jacob" [Ps. 81]; on the sixth day they sang "The Lord is king, and hath put on glorious apparel" [Ps. 93]. On the Sabbath they sang "A Psalm: A Song for the Sabbath Day" [Ps. 92]. (*Tamid* 7.4.)

[6] Mowinckel's analysis suggests that some private psalms were 'recited in small groups in ancient Israel, outside of Temple worship' (Mowinckel, *The Psalms in Israel's Worship*, 2:88).

[7] Stuhlmueller 1:44-45.

that the Song of Moses (Exod. 15.1-18) was one of those songs employed in Temple worship.[1] Besides these longer songs, various hymnic fragments appear throughout the Old Testament.[2] These might well be remnants of the 'new hymns' that the psalmist insists one need sing to the Lord.[3] According to the Mishnah, the daily Temple services also included a prayer service celebrated by the priests.[4] This service would have included the recitation of the decalogue, the *shema*, a series of benedictions, a psalm and a blessing over the people. While the Mishnah envisions that most of these prayer-elements were chanted by the priests, it is also probable that—to the extent that such a daily service existed— the Levites and even the ordinary Jews in attendance participated. Whatever the exact nature of the divergent texts employed in Temple worship, Werner believes that the psalmists' exhortation to 'sing to the Lord a new song' is clear evidence that a change in the musical repertoire was nothing new for the Levites in service of the Temple.[2]

SONG FORMS

Since we do not know much about the texts that were sung in Temple worship, it is difficult to outline with exactitude the accompanying musical forms. However, there are some recognizable structures embedded in existing texts as well as some 'stage directions' in the Old Testament that offer hints about the musical forms of Temple song.

Some Temple music undoubtedly included the voice of the people along with those of the musical specialists. Stuhlmueller's analysis of psalm 44, for example, suggests how individual singers, a choir and a larger assembly could have joined together in this hymn.[6] Psalm 136, the only Old Testament psalm with a refrain

---

[1] *Sotah* 5.4.
[2] For example Jer. 20.13 or Amos 4.13, 5.8-9, 9.5-6 as noted in Stuhlmueller 1:47.
[3] Pss. 33.3; 96.1; 98.1; 144.9; 149.1.
[4] *Tamid* 5.1; see the discussion of this service in Allan Bouley, *From Freedom to Formula*, The Catholic University of America Studies in Christian Antiquity 21 (The Catholic University of America Press, Washington DC, 1981), pp.7-13.
[5] Werner, *IDB* 3:463a.
[6] *Vv. 1-8: Hymnic Introduction*
    vv. 1-2: Call to praise, sung by everyone
    v. 3: Motivation, sung by large choir
    v. 4: sung by individual cantor or special choir
    v. 6: sung by individual cantor or special choir
    v. 8: choral refrain by everyone
  Vv. 9-16: Community Lament
    v. 15: sung by individual cantor or choir
    vv. 17-22 Reflection, sung by different choirs who
        vv. 17-19 speak to God
        vv. 20-21 speak about God
        v. speak to God. [Stuhlmueller 1:234].

after every colon,[1] offers another example of how amateur voices joining on this refrain might have blended with professional musicians in Temple song. The Mishnah 'remembers' a responsorial form in which the congregation responded to each verse with some brief refrain.[2] In a similar way, the assembly might have punctuated other psalms with cries of 'Hallelujah'.[3] It appears, therefore, that a variety of forms that divided the music between the professional musicians and the ordinary worshippers were employed in Temple worship.[4] It is also possible that some psalms (or sections of psalms) were divided amongst groups of Levitical singers, who alternated texts between them.[5]

Other psalms or sacred song texts could have been rendered strophically. The existence of strophic forms is suggested by the structure of psalms such as 119. This—the longest psalm in the Hebrew Scriptures—is comprised of 176 lines, grouped in 22 stanzas of 8 lines each.[6] The symmetry of the text intimates a similar symmetry in the song structure, that is, a strophic form. While there is no evidence that this particular psalm was employed in Temple worship, its presence within the psalter suggests the existence of strophic forms within the tradition of Jewish cultic song. Werner proposes that the form of many longer canticles or psalms 'must have been strophic, as without any such repetition . . . it was not possible to keep together the vocal and instrumental ensemble.'[7] It is also possible that some psalms or sacred songs were rendered as through-composed works.[8]

---

[1] John S. Kselman and Michael Barré, 'Psalms' in *NJBC* 34:153. For a further discussion of the evidence of 'refrains' in the psalms, see Alfred Sendry, *Music in Ancient Israel* (Philosophical Library, New York, 1969), pp.173-4.

[2] Speaking of the song in Exodus, the Mishnah comments, 'It teaches us that Israel made answer to everything after Moses, like as when they recited the *Hallel*' (*Sotah* 5.4, also *Sukkah* 3.10).

[3] for example, Psalms 146-150.

[4] In discussing the origins of the various forms of Jewish psalmody, Hanoch Avenary notes, 'The various kinds of Jewish psalmody arose from one formal principle: the confrontation of soloist and choir (responsorial psalmody)' (Hanoch Avenary, 'Formal Structure of Psalms and Canticles in Early Jewish and Christian Chant' in *Musica Disciplina* 7 (1953) 3).

[5] See, for example, the alternating structure in Ps. 103.20-22; such alternation, as Gelineau points out, is rooted in a parallelism endemic to Semitic poetry, in which the literary form of certain psalms is an 'invitation to dialogue' (Joseph Gelineau, 'Les formes de la psalmodie chrétienne' in *La Maison-Dieu* 33 (1953) p.163).

[6] The organizational principle here is the Hebrew alphabet of 22 letters; each stanza (and every line of that stanza) begins with a different letter of the Hebrew alphabet, so that all 22 letters have a complete stanza, in order of the alphabet (Stuhlmueller 2:152).

[7] Werner, 'Music' in *IDB* 3:463.

[8] A psalm such as 117, for example, is brief enough to have had its own melody, easily memorized, and tied only to this text.

INSTRUMENTS

While there are at least nineteen identifiable terms for musical instruments in the First Testament[1], not all of these instruments were regularly used in Temple worship. Some, like the ḥazozerah (trumpet), were frequently employed in Temple worship and 'the sounding of the trumpet was to be the duty and privilege of the Aaronite priests who exercised it both in war (2 Chron. 13.12) and in sacred ceremonies (Num. 10.8).'[2] Other instruments, such as the very popular tof[3]—although used to accompany religious ecstasy (1 Sam. 10.15) and songs of divine praise (Ps. 81.3)—were not played in the Temple, at least by the time it was populated by professional musicians.[4] In general, one can suggest that instrumental music in the second Temple was limited to trumpet flourishes, a large body of string instruments and a small number (or even single pair) of cymbals.[5] Instruments seems to have played an even more reduced role in the music of the first Temple.[6]

---

[1] While various scholars calculate these numbers differently, and offer various descriptions of such instruments, we produce here the relatively comprehensive yet conservatively described list of Bayer, plus a single biblical reference for each instrument: 1) *Asor* (Ps. 33.2), perhaps a small *Nevel* with only ten strings, 2) *Ḥalil* (1 Sam. 10.5), double-pipe wind instrument, 3) *Ḥazozerah* (Hos. 5.8), trumpet, made of precious metal, generally silver, 4) *Kaitros/Katros* (Dan. 3.5), Aramaic term for the Greek string instrument known as the *kithera*, 5) *Keren* (Josh. 6.5), probably another term for the *shofar*, 6) *Kinnor* (Ps. 150.3), string instrument of the lyre family, constituted by a body, two arms and a yoke, 7) *Mashrokita* (Dan. 3.5), Aramaic term for a whistling or piping instrument employed in the court of the Babylonian king, 8) *Mena'ane'im* (2 Sam. 6.5), possibly a pottery rattle, 9) *Meziltayim* (Ezra 3.10), *Zilzalim* (2 Sam. 6.5), *Mezillot* (Zech. 14.20), the first two forms probably stand for cymbals, while the third 'instrument' probably consists of metal ball-jingles, 10) *Minnim* (Ps. 150.5), an unclear term, presumably a string instrument, perhaps a lute, 11) *Nevel* (Ps. 150.3), a type of lyre, larger than the kinnor and, therefore, of deeper tone, 12) *Pa'amon* (Exod. 28.33), bells (originally metal platelets?) attached to the tunic of the High Priest, 13) *Pesanterin* (Dan. 3.5), Aramaic term for the Greek string instrument known as the *psalterion*, 14) *Sabbekha* (Dan. 3.5), Aramaic term for the Greek (string?) instrument known as the *sambyke*, 15) *Shalishim* (1 Sam. 18.6), possibly cymbals or struck metal bowls, 16) *Shofar* (1 Chr. 15.28), horn of the ram or a wild ovine, probably identical with the *keren*, 17) *Sumponyah* (Dan. 3.5), although sometimes identified as a 'bagpipe' (e.g. NAB), this Aramaic term is probably not a reference to a specific instrument but parallels the Greek *symphoneia*, which in itself means only 'the sounding together,' 18) *Tof* (2 Sam. 6.5), a shallow round frame drum, and 19) *Ugav* (Gen. 4.21), unclear but very probably not the wind instrument that medieval exegesis suggested, it could have been a harp. (Bathja Bayer, 'Music' in *EJ* 12:560).

[2] D. A. Foxvog and A. D. Kilmer, *Music* in *International Standard Bible Encyclopedia*, ed. Geoffrey Bromiley, 4 vols. (Wm. Eerdmans, Grand Rapids, 1986), 3:439.

[3] It is mentioned 17 times in the Old Testament, see Werner, 'Music', in *IDB* 3:474.

[4] In the case of the *tof*, this is possibly because the *tof* was played mainly by women (e.g. Exod. 15.20; Judg. 11.35, 1 Sam. 18.6, etc.) who assumed no role amongst the Temple's professional musicians.

[5] Bayer, 'Music' in *EJ* 12:560; as to the specific instruments employed in the Temple, the Mishnah mentions the *kinnor, nevel, ḥazozerah, meziltayim, zilz, the shofar* and the *ḥalil* (*Arakhin* 2.3 & 5).

[6] Bayer calls it 'minimal' (*Ibid.*).

The lack of surety about the number and identity of musical instruments in the First Testament hints at an even greater confusion about the usage of such instruments in Temple worship. Little is known for certain concerning instrumental performance practices in the Temple of any age. Given the types of instruments that probably were played in this worship, it is possible to suggest that instrumental music in the Temple was used either for signalling purposes or to accompany vocal music. The *ḥazozerah*, for example, probably produced a relatively high and shrill sound[1] that was more appropriate for signalling the entrance of ministers or announcing a sacrifice (Num. 10.10) than accompanying the human voice. The evidence that these instruments were virtually always used in pairs or even larger groupings[2] as well as the numerous examples from the First Testament and the New Testament underscore this 'signalling' usage.[3] There appears to have been no independent instrumental music apart from this signalling function.

Instruments were employed to accompany the Levitical song. These were most probably string instruments (Amos 5.23), possibly percussion and the very occasional use of a woodwind.[4] Werner suggests that 'the instrumental accompaniment was probably heterophonic, i.e. it reproduced the vocal line in an instrumental unison with slight melismatic deviations.'[5]

SUMMARY ON TEMPLE MUSIC
The paucity of clear information about the music of the Temple allows only the most general of conclusions.[6] Although probably not present at its inception, professional musicians soon came to dominate the Temple's music. In the relatively expansive musical vocabulary of the Jews, the terms for vocal music far outnumber the purely instrumental ones.[7] One can surmise that vocal music rather than instrumental similarly dominated. Instruments, apart from their signalling role, probably served to support the vocal music. While there may have been some instances of solo performance, it was not the norm

[1] See Werner, 'Musical Instruments' in *IDB* 3:472.
[2] 'In twenty-eight of its twenty-nine occurrences, zhazozerah appears in the plural, and it can be assumed that the trumpets were sounded in pairs or in larger ensembles, both to magnify their effect and to fulfill the command of Num. 10.2.' (Foxvog and Kilmer, 'Music' 3:440).
[3] e.g. Num. 10.2; 1 Chron. 15.24; Rev. 8-11.
[4] Werner suggests that, especially for solo singing, 'a highly differentiated accompaniment without a blending of the various timbres is desired, and for choral singing (with woodwind instruments, harps or lyres and percussion), sharp, high-pitched, rhythmically accentuated sounds' (Werner, 'Jewish Music,' in *NGDMM* 9:620).
[5] Werner, 'Instrumental Music,' in *IDB* 3:463.
[6] The sound of this music is even more problematic that its structure, texts, or the identity of the musicians. In this pre-notation period there was no accurate way to notate musical sound and preserve it for posterity. There have been many attempts to reconstruct the various modes and melodies that served as the building blocks for ancient Jewish music (for example, Idelsohn in *Jewish Music*). The speculative and technical nature of such reconstructions, however, do not recommend that we pursue the topic here.
[7] Werner, 'Music,' in *IDB* 3:460.

and choral music seem to have dominated.[1] The singing of religious texts appears to have followed the offering of sacrifices (2 Chron. 29.20-30) and trumpet blasts often accompanied the sacrifices (Num. 10.10). Latter rabbinic literature[2] as well as the writings of Josephus (d. ca. 100)[3] further note the connection between instrumental music and sacrifice in the Temple. In a latter period the Talmud taught that the lack of singing invalidated the sacrificial act.[4] This limited information suggests to Eric Werner that all music of the Temple, regardless of the period, was nothing but an accessory to its sacrificial ritual.[5] In this sacrificial context, the professional Levitical musicians dominated the musical landscape.[6]

THE INFLUENCE OF TEMPLE MUSIC ON CHRISTIAN PRACTICE
Practice Jesus' entire life was framed by Temple experiences. Eight days after his birth he was presented for circumcision in the Temple (Luke 2.21) and while he was on the cross the Temple veil was rent in two (Matt. 27.51). Jesus is remembered as having traveled to the Temple as a child, especially during the great pilgrim feasts such as Passover (Luke 2.41). As an adult he frequented the Temple during his public ministry. It was there that he prayed, taught, cured the sick and challenged contemporary religious practice (Matt. 21.12, 14). After his resurrection, the disciples continued to worship and evangelize in the Temple precincts (Acts 2.46; 3.1-11; 21.26). Although the Temple was a place of increasing tension for the disciples as they distinguished themselves from other Jews, the early Jewish Christians never completely rejected the Temple or its worship. On the other hand, Temple sacrifice, which was essential to Jewish cult, became increasingly peripheral for emerging Christianity, especially with the mission to the gentiles. The destruction of the Temple in 70 CE was undoubtedly a great blow to the Jewish Christian community, although the effect of its destruction on the ritual practices of Jewish Christians is less clear.

Temple music exerted little direct influence on the music of emerging Christianity. Professional guilds of musicians, instrumental accompaniment, and music designed for sacrifice were foreign to the early Christian experience.[7] On the other hand, Temple practice did announce that music played a central role at the very heart of the Jewish cult. Thus, the music of the Temple, as part of the sonic landscape of Jewish cult, contributed to the awareness in emerging Christianity that worship was, by its very nature, a lyric event.

---

[1] Werner, 'Jewish Music,' in *NGDMM* 9:622.

[2] The Mishnah and Talmud, for example, usually identify various musical activities by making reference to specific sacrifices (*Arakhin* 2:3-6; *B. Arakhin* 11a; *Tamid* 7:3-4; *B. Ta'anith* 27a).

[3] *Antiquities of the Jews* 7.12.3; also *Jewish War* 11.9.15; 15.8.1; 3.777; 9.4.2.

[4] *B. Arakin* 11a.

[5] Werner, 'Music' in *IDB* 3:459.

[6] In one of his last published works, Werner went even further in drawing the connection between the institution of sacrifice, hierarchy and professional or 'art' music. (*The Sacred Bridge* 2:149ff.).

[7] It is somewhat ironic that these musical elements re-emerged in Christianity after it had wed itself to the empire in the 4th century.

3. Synagogues of the First Century CE

THE SETTING

Unlike the Temple, the origins of the Jewish synagogue are yet in doubt. As Joseph Gutmann summarizes[1], there are three major theories current among scholars to explain the origins of the synagogue. Most scholars subscribe to the theory that the synagogue emerged during the Babylonian exile. A second group of scholars favour the Deuteronomic origin of the synagogue. Finally, a small group holds for a Hellenistic beginning of the synagogue in the third century BCE. According to Gutmann, however, the bases for all three theories are a faulty semantic analysis and inadequate historical conceptualization.[2] Firm literary evidence for the existence of the synagogue is extant only from the first century CE, specifically in the writings of Philo (d. ca. 50 CE)[3], Josephus (d. ca. 100 CE)[4] and the New Testament.[5] Archaeological evidence from the first century is neither as plentiful nor as firm.[6] This lack of literary and archaeological evidence combined with other historical and theological factors leads Gutmann to suggest that the synagogue arose only in the second century BCE.[7]

The re-evaluation of the origins of the synagogue, especially in view of extant archaeological evidence, has led scholars to re-evaluate the various theories about the architecture of primitive synagogues. With increasing frequency, the dominant 'evolutionary' theory—that there was an early Galilean prototype synagogue from which other synagogue types evolved in clear-cut, chronological

---

[1] Joseph Gutmann, 'Synagogue Origins: Theories and Facts, Ancient Synagogues' in *The State of Research*, Brown Judaic Studies 22, ed. Jacob Neusner et al. (Scholars Press, Chico CA, 1981), p.1.

[2] Gutmann, pp.2-3.

[3] for example, his *Life of Moses* 3:27.

[4] for example, his *Jewish War* (ca. 77-78 CE) 2:285, 289; 7:44, and his *Antiquities of the Jews* (ca. 94 CE) 19:300, 305.

[5] As a reference to the Jewish building, the word *'synagogē'* occurs 8 times in Mark, 9 times in Matthew, 15 times in Luke, twice in John and 16 times in the Acts of the Apostles. For a complete discussion of these references, see Wolfgang Schrage, 'synagogē', in *TDNT* 8:830-838.

[6] See Marilyn Chiat, 'First Century Synagogues: Methodological problems' in *Ancient Synagogues: The State of Research*, pp.49-60. In a subsequent volume, Chiat surveys the various archaeological sites that have been identified as ancient synagogues and suggests that to only two (Jerusalem: dated to the first century of this era p.202; and Herodium: stage I dated to the period following Herod's victory in 40 BCE p.207) can be ascribed a first century existence on the basis of archaeological evidence. (Marilyn Joyce Segal Chiat, *Handbook of Synagogue Architecture*, Brown Judaic Studies 29 (Scholars Press, Chico CA, 1982)). L. Michael White contends that the synagogue on Delos is probably the oldest. White believes that a private house was renovated for communal use in two stages (the late second century BCE and mid-first century BCE) (*idem*, 'The Delos Synagogue Revisited' in *Harvard Theological Review* 80 (1987) 133-60).

[7] Gutmann, pp.3-4.

stages—is giving way to the more complex theory of the coexistence of many types of synagogues in the early period.[1] Such a shift allows one to offer few generalizations about the physical setting of the first century CE synagogue.

Seager suggests that the earliest synagogues were simple structures without much elaboration in their plan, whereas later synagogues tended to be more highly differentiated, possibly reflecting an evolving interest in ritual and liturgy.[2] For example, the Torah was given an increasingly prominent setting as Scripture became more important to the community. In some cases a fixed repository for the Torah was a later addition to an already existing and functioning synagogue. While of varying sizes and shapes, early synagogues did tend to be relatively open structures. Sometimes a synagogue was orientated toward Jerusalem, and sometimes it was not.

SYNAGOGUE 'MUSICIANS'

It is especially when speaking about the synagogue that our modern distinction between music and public speech blurs. The presence of choirs and orchestras in the Temple allows us to speak with some clarity about its 'music' and, by consequence, to speak about Temple musicians. Such is more difficult, however, when discussing the synagogue. As a place where prayers were offered and the word was proclaimed, the synagogue was devoid of instrumental or choral music properly speaking. The performance of synagogal, word-centred worship, continuously migrated back and forth between what we might call speech and song.[3] While it was virtually always lyrical, in the broad sense of that term[4], the modern hearer (especially from Western cultures) might not always classify it as

---

[1] See the summary in Marilyn Chiat and Marchita Mauk, 'Using Archaeological Sources' in *Two Liturgical Traditions*, Vol. I: *The Making of Jewish and Christian Worship*, eds. Paul Bradshaw and Lawrence Hoffman (University of Notre Dame Press, New York, 1991), pp.69-80.

[2] Andrew Seager, 'Ancient Synagogue Architecture: An Overview' in *Ancient Synagogues: The State of Research*, p.41; much of what follows relies upon Seager's summary.

[3] As Jean-Jacques Nattiez notes, 'Examining the boarders between music and other symbolic forms along a given continuum reveals that the semantic surface of the concept "music" is displaced from one culture to another. This is particularly clear in societies [like ancient Israel] for which the word "music" does not exist'. Jean-Jacques Nattiez, *Music and Discourse: Toward a Semiology of Music*, trans. Carolyn Abbate (Princeton University Press, Princeton, 1990), p.54.

[4] Many cultures, like ancient Israel, 'do not in general have a term for music as a global phenomenon. Instead, they often have words that designate individual musical activities or artifacts, those who sing or play, songs, secular and religious, dance, and other more obscure categories'. (Hiromi Lorraine Sakata, *Music in the Mind: The Concepts of Music and Musicians in Afghanistan* (Kent State University Press, Kent, 1983), p.19). We will employ the word 'lyrical' throughout this work as a bridge term that, on the one hand, respects the ambiguity of the nature of what we might want to call 'music' in ancient Israel or emerging Christianity, and at the same time finds some resonance in the broad range of our own experiences of 'music.'

FIGURE 2. SYNAGOGUE AT SARDIS

Synagogue at Sardis, originally built as a Roman basilica (first century CE). In the foreground is the apse with three rows of benches for the elders of the community. Beyond the apse is the marble table, probably used for the reading of Torah. Toward the back of the hall are the bases of four pillars, which may have supported the reader's desk. At the far end are three entrances with shrines between them, which may have been used for storing the Torah scrolls. Text and illustration after Geoffrey Wigoder, *the Story of the Synagogue* (Harper & Row, San Francisco, 1986), pp.32-33.

musical.[1] This musical ambiguity is underscored by the absence of identifiable musicians in the synagogue for the first centuries of its existence.

As I have suggested before[2], the absence of an identifiable musician or even fixed prayer leader in the synagogue is wed to an approach to prayer leadership that was decidedly more 'democratic' than that found in the Temple.[3] As Idelsohn notes, 'In Judaism the idea became prevalent, through the influence of the prophets, that God is near to everybody, and that everybody is worthy of approaching [God]. The relationship between God and Israel, as between [parent] and children, entitled everyone to pray to God without priestly mediation.'[4] Heinemann further asserts that the rise of statutory prayer in the period of the Second Temple heralds the 'democratization of the divine worship' with a new form of worship 'to be performed by each individual, by the entire community of worshippers, wherever they may be.'[5] This perspective had a marked influence on the emerging synagogue that was devoid of a professional priesthood.

Because of the unique Jewish perspective on prayer leadership, the execution of the synagogue service was not relegated to an ordained or permanent clergy,[6] and through Talmudic and early Gaonic times, volunteers functioned as leaders of the service.[7] Such a volunteer was already in the oldest sources called *sheliach*

---

[1] For a contemporary example of this distinction, see Gordon Thompson's discussion of the Cāran, some of whom identify their performances as musical, some as non-musical, in 'The Cārans of Gujarat: Caste Identity, Music and Cultural Change' in *Ethnomusicology* 35 (1991) 388-389.

[2]. See my 'The Cantor in Historical Perspective' in *Worship* 56 (1982) 194-213.

[3] One witness to democratic prayer leadership in the history of Judaism is reflected in an institution which some believe to be of considerable influence in the development of the synagogue. The *ma'amadot* (lit. 'standing me' or bystanders) was a second Temple division of the Israelites into twenty-four groups or watches. Each *ma'amadot*, in weekly rotations, sent representatives to the Temple to 'stand by' the priests and levites during the daily sacrifices. Since only a representative group (*anshe ma'amadot*) was allowed to attend, the rest of the *ma'amadot* 'stood by' at home, where, in union with their representatives in Jerusalem, they fasted, prayed, and read those sections of the Torah which related to sacrifice. See S. Zeitlin, 'The Origin of the Synagogue' in *Studies in the early History of Judaism* I (Ktav Publishing House, New York, 1973), p.77.

[4] Idelsohn, *Jewish Music*, pp.101-102.

[5] Joseph Heinemann, *Prayer in the Talmud*, trans. Richard Sarason, Studia Judaica 9 (Walter De Gruyter, Berlin-New York, 1977), p.14.

[6] 'It is true that the priest is the first to read from the Torah, but it would seem that this custom derives from the priest's ancient role as teacher of Torah to the people. There is, however, no *halakah* which grants him preferential privileges in conducting public worship, such as leading the *amidah* or the reading of the *shema*. Nor is being a priest enumerated among the desirable characteristics which a prayer leader should possess (as in *Taanith* 3.2)' (Heinemann, *Prayer in the Talmud*, p.117, n. 30).

[7] See Lawrence Hoffman, *The Canonization of the Synagogue Service*, Notre Dame Center for the Study of Judaism and Christianity in Antiquity 4 (University of Notre Dame Press, Notre Dame-London, 1979), pp.103-105, and *passim*.

tsibbur (literally 'the emissary of the people').[1] These volunteers were sometimes chosen by the elder of the synagogue—the *rosh ha-knesset* or *archisunagogos*—a kind of superintendent who was responsible for overseeing the worship and maintaining order.[2] That the *sheliach tsibbur* could be any member of the congregation is demonstrated by the fact that even women were sometimes selected to mediate in the name of the community.[3] While it is true that standards for selecting the *sheliach tsibbur* emerged by the end of the second century[4]—and that, with increasing frequency, vocal ability became a determining factor in selecting the honorary precentor[5]—there is no such evidence from the first century CE. Prayer leadership in the synagogues of that era was not conceived first and foremost as a musical role, and there was no separate or distinctive musician in the first century synagogue.[6]

---

[1] Ismar Elbogen, *Der jüdische Gottesdienst in seiner Entwicklung* (G. Fock, Leipzig, 1913; reprint. 1962), p.488.

[2] Elbogen, *Gottesdienst*, p.483; for a more recent study of this role, see Bernadette Brooten, *Women Leaders in the Ancient Synagogue*, Brown Judaic Studies 36, ed. Jacob Neusner et al. (Scholars Press, Chico CA, 1982), pp.5-33; also Schrage, '*archisynagogos*' in *TDNT* 8:844-847.

[3] Abraham Z. Idelsohn, *Jewish Liturgy and Its Development* (Schocken Books, New York, 1960 [1932]), p.102; also, Brooten who, although not specifically treating the role of the *sheliach tsibbur*, does comment: 'Seen in the larger context of women's participation in the life of the ancient synagogue, there is no reason not to take the titles [archēgos (leader), elder, mother of synagogue, and priest] as functional, nor to assume that women heads or elders of synagogues had radically different functions than men heads or elders of synagogues. Of the functions outlined for each title, there are none which women could not have carried out.' (p.149). That this perspective was to change radically is illustrated by Rav's harsh statement from the Talmud, 'The voice of a woman is indecency' (B. *Berakoth* 24a).

[4] The Mishnah, for example, reports: 'They arise for prayer. They bring down before the ark an experienced elder, who has children and whose cupboard house is empty, so that his heart should be wholly in the prayer. And he says before them 24 blessings: the eighteen said every day, and he adds six more to them' (*Taanith* 2.2). A list of such qualifications was fixed by Rabbi Judah ben Illai in the second century AD., which required the emissary to be 'a man who has heavy family obligations, who has not enough to meet them, who has to struggle for a livelihood but who nonetheless keeps his house clean, who has an attractive appearance, is humble, pleasant to and liked by people, who has a sweet voice and musical ability, who is well versed in the Scriptures, capable of preaching, conversant with the *halakah* and *haggadah* and who knows all the prayers and benedictions by heart' (B. *Taanith* 16a).

[5] See the summary of this evidence in my 'The Cantor in Historical Perspective', pp.198-199.

[6] There is some Talmudic evidence for certain levitical singers moving back and forth between Temple and synagogue (e.g. B. *Sukkah* 53a) that Werner interprets as a movement to 'transfer the tradition of the central sanctuary to the country synagogue' (*Sacred Bridge*, vol. I (Schocken Books, New York, 1970 (1959), p.24). Talmudic evidence for first century CE practice greatly weakens the credibility of such an assertion, although one could not rule out completely the possible cross-fertilization between Temple and synagogue. The role of professional Temple singers in the synagogue could not, however, be considered normative in any sense of the word.

SYNAGOGUE 'SONG'

While Temple worship revolved around sacrifice, synagogue services centred on the recitation of various texts. Establishing the various texts or kinds of texts employed in first century synagogues will enable us to explore something of their lyricism and their lyrical forms.

The Statutory Prayers: In his classic study on the history of Jewish prayer, Joseph Heinemann asserts that the institution of fixed, communal prayer constitute a 'radical innovation of the Second Temple period.'[1] Considered on a par with the sacrificial cult of the Temple, such obligatory and fixed prayer was understood as a legitimate form of divine worship, through which Israel fulfilled its daily communal obligations to the Lord.[2] Such prayers, oral at their root, were improvised from their inception. Eventually a common repertoire of frequently employed idioms and fixed formulae begin to define these prayers which, in general, could be considered ' "free-style" prayer.'[3] The oldest such prayer is the *shema*[4], which is really more of a profession of faith than a prayer. The *shema* has traditionally been surrounded by a series of benedictions.[5] While it is not possible to establish with any certainty when these prayers appeared, the Mishnah already notes their existence, and does so in such a way as to suggest that the *shema* and 'its benedictions' are a well-established unit.[6] Another statutory prayer is the eighteen benedictions or *amidah*, that antedated the destruction of Herod's Temple 'by a considerable period of time'.[7] These two prayer elements, at least, were central to the synagogue services of the first century CE.[8]

---

[1] Heinemann, *Prayer in the Talmud*, p.14.

[2] *Ibid.*

[3] *Ibid.*, pp.64-65.

[4] composed of three biblical texts: Deut. 6.4-9; 11.13-21; Num. 15.37-41.

[5] As Elbogen notes, 'The bare recitation of a profession of faith is too meagre to make up, for any length of time, the only element of a congregational service. It is therefore quite natural that the Biblical sections were enframed in an harmonious introduction and conclusion.' (Ismar Elbogen, 'Studies in the Jewish Liturgy I' in *Jewish Quarterly Review* 19 (1907) 233).

[6] *Berakoth* 1.4; *Megillah* 4.3, 5. Josephus notes that the *shema* is recited twice each day in his *Antiquities of the Jews* 4.18.13. On the antiquity of the *shema* as a liturgical unit, see Elbogen, *Gottesdienst*, p.25; this view is challenged by Tzvee Zahavy, who holds for the later emergence of the *shema* as a 'popular scribal rite', in his 'The Politics of Piety' in *The Making of Jewish and Christian Worship*, pp.50-54.

[7] Heinemann, *Prayer in the Talmud*, p.22; he further suggests that the custom of reciting precisely eighteen benedictions must have crystallized sometime during the century before the destruction of the Temple (at the very latest), p.224; for a different perspective, see Zahavy who suggests that 'this prayer formed the core of the priestly liturgy sponsored by the patriarchate after the destruction of the Temple' (p.57).

[8] Zahavy is more cautious, suggesting that 'during the initial transition after the destruction of the Temple from about 70 to 90 CE the priests promulgated the *tefillah* and the scribes promoted the *shema* . . .. In the second phase of development, from about 90 to 155 CE, the patriarchate sponsored the *tefillah* to counter a growing scribal faction within the rabbinic movement . . .. In the era from about 155 to 220 CE the rabbis amalgamated the *shema* and the *tefillah* in a compromise that led to the present shape of the composite rabbinic service.' (*Ibid.*, pp.61-62). For a more traditional view of these elements and their role in the first century synagogue, see Bouley, pp.13-28.

Readings: Publicly reading from both the Law (Torah) and the Prophets (Haftarah) was an ancient synagogue practice.[1] The Lukan passage describing Jesus' reading from the Prophet Isaiah in the synagogue at Nazareth underscores the established nature of such reading by reporting a series of well choreographed ritual actions and procedures surrounding such reading.[2] Other New Testament passages are explicit about the custom of publicly reading the prophets and the Torah in the synagogue.[3] It became customary—probably during the centuries preceding the destruction of the Temple—to follow the readings from the Law and the Prophets with a series of benedictions.[4] By the time of the Mishnah, the process of enumerating the number of readers and designating particular pericopes for each Sabbath and festival had already begun.[5] This process of standardization, however, did not occur in all places during the mishnaic period.[6]

Psalmody: It is often suggested that psalmody played a central role in synagogue worship at the dawn of Christianity.[7] Such is not, however, demonstrable from the earliest sources.[8] As Werner points out, for example, the Mishnah and Talmud are strangely silent about the commonly accepted linkage between scripture readings and psalmic responses.[9] Positing the existence of scripture readings in the first century CE synagogue service, therefore, does not prove the presence of psalmody—except, perhaps, as 'parts of the Holy Scripture, of the authorized and inspired canon, for reading, just like the other biblical books, which were read in the synagogues as holy words of God.'[10] Beginning certain services with the recitation of psalms[11] is also a late development, unattested to in

---

[1] Heinemann, *Prayer in the Talmud*, p.25.

[2] i.e., the scroll of the prophet Isaiah was handed to Jesus (Luke 4.17), possibly by the assistant who retrieved the scroll from him in 4.20a; he chose a passage (4.17a); he read the passage; he rolled up the scroll (4.20); he handed the scroll back to the assistant (4.20); he offered a teaching (4.21).

[3] e.g. Acts 13.27 referring to the former; Acts 15.21 and 1 Cor. 3.15 referring to the latter.

[4] Heinemann, *Prayer in the Talmud*, pp.228-229.

[5] See, for example, *Megillah* 3.4-6; 4.1-2.

[6] See Joseph Heinemann, 'The Triennial Lectionary Cycle' in *Journal of Jewish Studies*, 19 (1968) 41-48.

[7] See, for example, Anton Arens, *Die Psalmen im Gottesdienst des Alten Bundes. Eine Untersuchung zur Urgeschichte des christlichen Psalmengesanges*, Triere theologische Studien 11 (Paulinus Verlag, Trier, 1961), esp. pp.160-202.

[8] See the useful summary in Massey Shepherd, *The Psalms in Christian Worship* (Liturgical Press, Collegeville, 1976), p.26.

[9] Werner, *The Sacred Bridge* 1:131.

[10] Mowinckel, *The Psalms in Israel's Worship* 1:88.

[11] For example, the service 'Welcoming the Sabbath' from the traditional Siddur, begins with Psalms 95-99 and 29. See *Prayerbook for Sabbath and Festivals*, trans. and annotated by Philip Birnbaum (Hebrew Publishing Company, New York, 1950), pp.24-30.

the earliest data. While it is true that the recitation of certain psalms as part of the morning service comes from at least the second century, this was apparently an optional custom.[1] For his part, Heinemann gives no attention to psalmody *per se* in his discussion of statutory elements of synagogue worship.[2] While the spirit of prayer embodied in the psalms may have influenced synagogal prayer in the first century CE—suggested by the incorporation of various psalm phrases into the standard benedictions, and even the composition of new psalm-like compositions for common worship[3]—it is questionable whether psalms were ordinarily sung in first century synagogue worship. Rather, as Johann Maier summarizes, the psalms were valued first of all as biblical texts, not as a collection of songs.[4]

'SONG' FORMS

As previously noted, there is more surety about the form of ancient Jewish prayer forms than there is about their melodic or rhythmic structure. We will, therefore, concentrate on the former and offer a few reflections on the latter.

The Statutory Prayers: The creedal nature of the *shema* suggests that every Jew knew this profession of faith by heart—a suggestion bolster by the pointed biblical injunction to 'drill' these words into every child and to 'mark' body and home with them.[5] It is possible, therefore, that at an early stage, the *shema* could have been chanted in unison by the whole assembly during the service. Evidence from the earliest stage of the codification of the synagogue service, however, suggests that a *sheliach tsibbur* led the members of the congregation in the recitation of the *shema*: reciting the confession and its benedictions line by line from his/ her place, while the congregation repeated each line in course.[6] Either style would have required relatively simple musical settings for these congregational chants.

While the Mishnah does acknowledge that it was possible—even necessary— to pray the *amidah* every day, it simultaneously underscores the demanding

---

[1] Hoffman, *The Canonization of the Synagogue Service*, p.127.

[2] Heinemann, *Prayer in the Talmud*, ch. 9, 'The Fixed Statutory Prayers of the Synagogue' and *passim*.

[3] Philo comments, for example, that the synagogue was a place where the participants performed 'hymns, songs and canticles' (*Against Flaccum* 14). Although he provides no examples of what these might have looked like, see the *psalmi idiotici* composed by the Qumran community collected in Geza Vermes, *The Dead Sea Scrolls in English*, 2nd ed. (Penguin Books, Middlesex, 1975), pp.150-201.

[4] Johann Maier, 'Zur Verwendung der Psalmen in der synagogalen Liturgie' in *Liturgie und Dichtung: ein interdisziplinäres Kompendium*, eds. H. Becker and R. Kaczynski, 2 vols., *Pietas Liturgica* 1-2 (Sankt Ottilien: EOS-Verlag), 1:84.

[5] 'Take to heart these words which I enjoin on you today. Drill them into your children. Speak of them at home and abroad, whether you are busy or at rest. Bind them at your wrist as a sign and let them be a pendent on your forehead. Write them on the door-posts of your houses and on your gates.' (Deut. 6:6-9. Cf. Ps. 1.2).

[6] See the summary in Hoffman, *The Canonization of the synagogue Service*, p.47; also, Elbogen, 'Studies in the Jewish Liturgy II' in *Jewish Quarterly Review* 19 (1907) 709-711.

nature of this prayer.[1] Such is not only because of the length of the prayer, but also because of the fluid state of this prayer text. As Hoffman notes, 'though the prayer ... became a staple daily liturgical portion with specifically stipulated petitionary themes officially arranged in orderly sequence, there still remained great differences among the tannaim[2] as to the requisite number of blessings and the wording thereof. It may be that blessing topics were settled upon, and even some sample eulogies which seemed more representative of the prayer's basic intent than others. Yet even here it is hard to imagine a final and absolute crystallization until after the promulgation of the Mishnah.'[3]

Such would make the common recitation of the *amidah* by the whole assembly virtually impossible. Rather, the *amidah* was ordinarily led by the *sheliach tsibbur*[4], who improvised this series of benedictions according to increasingly standardized formulae; the assembly may have added some phrases of blessing or affirmation at least at the end of the prayer.[5]

Since these prayers were led by ordinary people—and sometimes echoed by the entire congregation—the prayer settings were, by necessity, simple. At the same time, the fluid nature of the evolving prayer texts dictated that such prayer settings were 'of a plastic and variable nature in order to be fitted to longer or shorter phrases of the prose texts without difficulty.'[6] In response to such need there developed certain 'prayer modes' (*nusahim*), probably based on already existent modes employed for chanting biblical texts.[7] As to the sound of these modes, Avenary summarizes, 'Although it is impossible to ascribe individual tunes heard today to the early synagogue with any degree of certainty, it is legitimate to speak of the principle of chanting according to a *nusah*.[8]

---

[1] *Berakoth* 4.4.

[2] The period of the tannaim can be said to have begun with the destruction of the Temple, ending with the redaction of the Mishnah, i.e. from 70 to ca. 200. See Neusner, *From Politics to Piety*, especially chs. 6 and 7.

[3] Hoffman, *The Canonization of the Synagogue Service*, p.50.

[4] Elbogen, 'Studies II' pp.709-710.

[5] Thus Heinemann comments, 'Although there were undoubtedly many people who were not fluent in the fixed prayers ... and who were thus necessarily dependent on hearing the prayers recited by the Prayer Leader in order to fulfill their obligation, nevertheless, their participation through listening was of an active nature, which found expression in the frequent responses: "Amen", "Blessed be the Lord to whom blessing is due forever and ever", "May his great name be eternally blessed," "Blessed be the name of his glorious kingdom for all eternity," etc.' in *Prayer in the Talmud*, p.16. Philo's description of the Therapeutae (*On the Contemplative Life* 10) offers evidence that responsorial forms were common at least in some sectors of Judaism at the time: 'Then the president rises and sings a hymn composed as an address to God, either a new one of his own composition or an old one by prophets of an earlier day .... while all the rest listen in complete silence except when they have to chant the closing lines or refrains, for then they all lift up their voices, men and women alike.' in *Philo*, 10 vols, The Loeb Classical Library, trans. F. H. Colson (Harvard University Press, Cambridge MA, 1941), 9:163.

[6] Avenary, 'Music' in *EJ* 12:578.

[7] Idelsohn, *Jewish Music*, p.73.

[8] Avenary, 'Music' in *EJ* 12:578; for some examples of contemporary prayer modes, thought to reflect traditional Jewish music, see *idem* 12:581.

The Readings: Specific evidence for chanting the readings from Torah and the prophets in the synagogue is imbedded in the Babylonian Talmud. This sixth century source 'remembers' teachings about chanted biblical texts from as early as the second century CE. For example, the Talmud reports that Rabbi Akiba (d. ca. 135 CE) stressed the necessity of daily chanting the scriptures when studying them.[1] It further reports that Rav (d. ca. 250 CE) interpreted a section of the book of Nehemiah (8.8) as a reference to 'punctuation by means of melodic cadences.'[2] The most celebrated passage of the Talmud about chanting the readings is ascribed to Johanan: 'He who reads the Torah without chant... of him can it be said as it is written, "the laws that I gave you were not good" (Ezek. 20.25).[3] Werner assesses this last saying with the comment, 'to recite scripture without chant was considered a minor sacrilege'.[4]

It is not possible to establish with certainty when this tradition of chanting the scriptures at synagogue services began. Given the previously elaborated profile about the acoustic environment of the ancient world in general, and ancient Judaism in particular, it would be difficult to imagine any public reading in the synagogue that was not fundamentally lyrical.[5] At the beginning of this tradition, this could simply have involved a heightened declamation of the text, or the employment of simple musical cadences which clarified the structure of each biblical sentence.[6] Eventually there seem to have developed distinctive modes or formulae for the chanting of various types of scripture, like the Law and the Prophets.[7] As the reading of the Torah and the Prophets became more central to the

---

[1] B. *Sanhedrin* 99a.

[2] Avenary, 'Music' in *EJ* 12:577, in reference to B. *Megillah* 3a.

[3] B. *Megillah* 32a.

[4] Werner, 'Jewish Music' in *NGDMM* 9:623.

[5] See Solange Corbin, *L'église à la conquête de sa musique*, Pour la Musique, ed. Roland-Manuel (Gallimard, Paris, 1960), p.42.

[6] Avenary, 'Jewish Music', 1:995. Werner distinguishes a threefold variety for publicly rendering readings: plain recitation (spoken), ecphonesis (*Sprechgesang*, or a semi-musical recitative) and cantillation (regular musical chant). Werner goes on to suggest that it is virtually impossible to distinguish between the last two forms. He concludes that 'the "primitive", acoustically unorganized rendering of Scripture is not easily accessible to musical evaluation and classification' (Werner, *Sacred Bridge* 1:104). This perspective is corroborated by Edith Gerson-Kiwi, who believes that cantillation is first of all amplification of the word employing a restricted number of sounds, governed by the verbal rhythm in phrases devoid of any metrical structure. Cantillation, therefore, is not a melodic ornament, and still less a genuine musical composition, since the text is pronounced rapidly to the degree of flexibility permitted by the nature of the language involved. Edith Gerson-Kiwi, 'Musique (dans la Bible): La lecture biblique (cantillation)', in *Dictionnaire de la Bible: supplément* (Paris, 1957), 5:1449-1464, as summarized in Giulio Cattin, *Music of the Middle Ages I*, trans. Steven Botterill (Cambridge University Press, Cambridge, 1984), p.8.

[7] For a discussion of some of these various modes as they occurred in more recent usage, see Idelsohn, *Jewish Music*, pp.35-91.

synagogue service[1]—especially after the destruction of the Temple—it became increasingly important to regulate the musical formulae and the use of such formulae when chanting the scriptures. As Avenary explains,

'Although the text of the Hebrew Bible was fixed long since, every sequence of words could become meaningful only by the correct grouping of the words and a clear interrelation of clauses and subclauses. The division of a verse could become a matter of interpretation, or even ideology, and raise debates with dissenting sects or a foreign creed. It was no wonder that in epochs of insecurity a need was felt to make the accepted infrastructure of biblical verses in an indisputable way—in writing.'[2]

That 'indisputable way' was the introduction of accents (te'amin) into the written text.[3] Sometimes called 'ekphonetic notation',[4] these accents appeared from the sixth century onward.[5] The most important set of these accents were developed by a group of scholars living in the ancient city of Tiberias by the end of the 9th century CE. This Tiberian system of notation—which, according to tradition, was invented by the family of Ben Asher—was imposed upon the whole of Jewry and is still in use.[6] While some scholars maintain that the Tiberian system was purely syntactical rather than musical[7], others believe that this system of accents reflects a musical system that developed before the emergence of Christianity that can be reconstructed today.[8] Most scholars do not believe, however, that a clear deciphering of the Tiberian system is possible, or that one can demonstrate an indisputable link between the Tiberian system and the most ancient traditions of biblical cantillation. A series of studies comparing current musical practice with transcriptions made since 1518[9] do suggest, however, that the continuity between ancient and modern synagogue musical practice—passed on through oral tradition—is quite strong.[10]

[1] The increased importance of the reading of the Torah seems to be demonstrated by architectural changes in the synagogue (Seager, 'Ancient Synagogue Architecture: An Overview,' p.43).

[2] Avenary, 'Music' in *EJ* 12:583.

[3] These accents seem to have replaced a series of conventional hand and finger gestures called chironomy that (until the introduction of written accents) had been the traditional way to signal the places for musical cadences in the texts. See Avenary, 'Jewish Music' 1:995.

[4] From the Greek *ekphōneō* to 'call out' or 'declaim'; the term was coined by Isaac Tzetzes, *Parnassos* ix (1885), p.441, as cited in Gudrun Engberg, *NGDMM* 6:99.

[5] Avenary, 'Music' in *EJ* 12:583. This phenomenon occurred at about the same time that Jewish scholars (Masoretes) began adding vowel symbols to the consonantal spelling that, until that time, had been used for writing Hebrew and other Semitic languages. The result of this process was the emergence of the Masoretic text of the Old Testament. See, for example, the introduction by H. M. Orlinsky, 'The Masoretic Text: Fact or Fiction' in the facsimile reprint of Christian David Ginsburg, *Introduction to the Massoretico-Critical Edition of the Hebrew Bible* (New York, 1966).

[6] See Avenary, 'Music' in *EJ* 12:584.

[7] Werner, 'Jewish Music' *NGDMM* 9:624.

[8] Suzanne Haik-Vantoura, *The Music of the Bible Revealed*, trans. Dennis Weber, ed. John Wheeler (Bibal Pres, Berkeley CA, 1991).

[9] See, for example, Hanoch Avenary, *The Ashkenazi Tradition of Biblical Chant between 1500 and 1900* (Tel-Aviv University, Tel-Aviv, 1978).

[10] Werner, 'Jewish Music' in *NGDMM* :624. The best single collection of transcriptions of various forms of cantillation continues to be that of Idelsohn, *Hebräisch-orientalischer Melodienschatz.*

The benedictions that followed the readings from the Law and the Prophets were likely chanted according to the previously discussed 'prayer modes'—improvised according to accepted patterns by the *sheliach tsibbur*, with the assembly adding some phrases of blessing or affirmation at least at the end of the prayer.

INSTRUMENTS

While the Temple was a place of instrumental music, the synagogue was not. Even before the destruction of the Temple in 70 CE there is little evidence to suggest that any instruments—possibly with the exception of the *shofar*—were ever used in the synagogue. After 70 CE only the *shofar* was employed in synagogue worship.[1] As to the abandonment of all other instrumental music in the synagogue, Werner offers this assessment:

> 'At the destruction of the Temple all instrumental music apart from that of the *shofar* was excluded from worship, partly because of the hostility of the Pharisees to such music, partly because of the deep mourning for the Temple and the land, and the disappearance of the levitical functions, including the provision of music for the sanctuary.... With the destruction of the Temple the hour of the rabbis struck. During the next five or six centuries they patched up a legal framework for the general prohibition of all instrumental music, from various and not always convincing arguments.... This exclusion of instruments from Jewish worship remained in force generally for many centuries; only at the loss of political power by the rabbis in the 19th century Emancipation did instrumental music once again appear in the (liberal) synagogue, and the exclusion still remains in force where, as in modern Israel, orthodox rabbis retain some power.'[2]

SUMMARY ON SYNAGOGUE MUSIC

While there is much about ancient synagogal music that we do not know, there are a number of basic assertions that we can make about this music—especially as contrasted with the music of the ancient Temple. While the music of the Temple was predominantly vocal, the music of the synagogue was exclusively vocal with a complete absence of instruments except the *shofar*, which never accompanied any vocalization but only served as a signal instrument.[3] In the Temple choral music seems to have dominated, while in the ancient synagogue there appears to have been much more individual or solo performance with responses by the congregation. While Eric Werner may assert that Temple music was nothing but an accessory to its sacrificial ritual[4], synagogue music was what

---

[1] Of the numerous references to the *shofar* in the Mishnah, only a few make specific reference to the use of the *shofar* in the synagogue, e.g., *Rosh ha-Shanah* 3.7; 4.5-9; and *Taanith* 2.3-4.

[2] Werner, 'Jewish Music' in *NGDMM* 9:623.

[3] Werner, 'Musical Instruments' in *IDB* 3:473.

[4] Werner, 'Music' in *IDB* 3:459.

Sachs called 'logogenic' or 'word-born'.[1] And this word-centred music belonged to non-professional, lay leadership—not the professional musicians and clergy who dominated the Temple. As to the style of this music, one must agree with Avenary who reckoned that synagogal styles were 'elementary ... suited to a gathering of people assembled for singing prayer and praise, and for the majority of whom artistically contrived song and complicated tunes were normally out of range. Such congregations had to be cemented together by a kind of music that was easily grasped and performed.'[2]

THE INFLUENCE OF SYNAGOGUE MUSIC IN CHRISTIAN PRACTICE

Jesus probably attended synagogue services while growing up in Nazareth.[3] Very early in his public ministry he is remembered as having visited the synagogues to pray.[4] It is also in the synagogue that he cast out demons[5], healed the sick[6], taught[7] and preached.[8] Not only is Jesus remembered as appearing in the synagogue, he is also remembered as having taken a role in synagogal worship—accepting the role of *sheliach tsibbur* for the community and reading from the scroll of Isaiah.[9] The statutory prayers of the synagogue service were so well known to him that he is remembered as having woven them into his teaching.[10] Furthermore, the specific model of prayer that Jesus handed on to his disciples[11] employs prayer idioms common in the synagogue[12], and suggests, again, his familiarity with that setting and its services.

Following the example of Jesus, the disciples continued to frequent the synagogues. There they preached, prayed, and spread the good news.[13] Paul is remembered as having preached his message first in the synagogue.[14] The presence of Jesus' followers was so evident in the synagogue that around the

---

[1] Curt Sachs, *The Rise of Music in the Ancient World* (W. W. Norton & Company, New York, 1943), p.52.

[2] Avenary, 'Music', *EJ* 12:571.

[3] Luke 4.16 notes that Jesus attended the synagogue in Nazareth 'according to his custom'; on the interpretation of this phrase in view of Jesus' upbringing, see Gustaf Hermann Dalman, *Jesus-Jeshua: Studies in the Gospels* (McMillan, New York, 1929), pp.33-34, 40.

[4] Luke 4.16.

[5] Mark 1.23-27 (Luke 4.33-36); Mark 1.39.

[6] Matt. 4.23; Mark 3.1-5 (Matt. 12.9-13; Luke 6.6-10); Matt. 9.35; Luke 13.10- 7.

[7] Matt. 4.23; Matt. 9.35; Luke 13.10.

[8] Mark 1.39; Matt. 9.35.

[9] Luke 4.16.

[10] for example, the section from the *shema* in Matt. 22.37.

[11] Luke 11.2-4=Matt. 6.9-13.

[12] Heinemann, *Prayer in the Talmud*, p.63; on the anti-synagogal' nature of the Lord's Prayer, however, see Joseph Heinemann, 'The Background of Jesus' Prayer in the Jewish Liturgical Tradition' in *The Lord's Prayer and Jewish Liturgy*, eds. Jakob Petuchowski and Michael Brocke (Crossroad Books, New York, 1978), pp.81-89.

[13] Acts 9.20; 13.5, 15; 14.1; 17.1, 10, 17; 18.4, 19, 26; 19.8.

[14] Acts 9.19-20.

year 80 CE the Jews introduced a malediction against these heretics.[1] This can be considered a significant marker in the relationship between Christians and Jews, and the beginning of the end of their worship together.

While it is also true that many followers of Jesus were also present in the Temple until its destruction, Temple cult had little direct influence on emerging Christian worship and song. The synagogue, on the other hand, influenced substantially emerging Christian life, worship and 'music'. This non-clerical, lay-led, word-centred worship—where a spiritualized sacrifice of praise occupied the heart of the worship—provided an important model to the followers of Jesus.[2] From a musical perspective, the synagogue was especially influential on the emerging Christian practice of public reading and public prayer texts.

---

[1] On the *birkat-ha-minim* see W. Horbury, 'The Benediction of the Minim and Early Jewish Christian Controversy' in *Journal of Theological Studies* 33 (1982) 19-61; as to whether or not this 'malediction' was directed specifically or exclusively at Christians, see Reuven Kimleman, '*Birkat Haminim* and the Lack of Evidence for an Anti-Christian Prayer in Late Antiquity' in *Jewish and Christian Self-Definition*, Vol. 2: *Aspects of Judaism in the Graeco-Roman Period*, eds. E. P. Sanders, A. I. Baumgarten, and Alan Mendelson (SCM Press, London, 1980), 2:226-44, 392-403.

[2] See, for example, my discussion of the Christian adaptation of the *sheliach tsibbur* in 'The Cantor in Historical Perspective', pp.202-204.

4. Borrowed Spaces and Emerging Christianity [the first century CE]

THE 'SETTING'

Unlike many religions of the surrounding region, ancient Israel did not restrict its worship to a single location or type of building. It is true that, until its destruction in 70 CE, the Temple was the centre of Jewish sacrifice, and synagogues became important centres for prayer and study by the second century BCE. Prayer was not confined, however, to these two institutions. A pious Jew was expected to pray in every place and at every time.[1] This meant that breaking bread, seeing lightning, purchasing a vessel or watching the sun set were all occasions for blessing God.[2] While virtually every and any location was an appropriate setting for offering a blessing, the home—like the Temple and synagogues—was a privileged place in ancient Judaism for prayer. This was especially true since the home was the central setting for meals which were always sacred events for Jews.

Jesus' table ministry can be considered one of the most characteristic acts of his ministry[3], as well as the context in which the disciples experienced Jesus as the Risen one.[4] Thus, it is appropriate to suggest that Christianity was born around the table. It is significant, however, that Christianity did not emerge around any single table, or in any particular kind of house or dwelling. There is— historically speaking—no aboriginal, 'mother-church' in Christianity. Rather, Christianity arose around many tables, in a variety of private and public settings.[5] Such is the model provided by Jesus himself, who moved from place to place and table to table. The diversity of the settings for his ministry are remarkable: homes of the rich, borrowed rooms, public inns, houses of tax collectors, and even grassy hillsides.[6] What is most notable is that none of them belonged to him.

---

[1] 'A man is obliged to recite one hundred benedictions each day.' (B. *Menahot* 43b).

[2] See, for example, the discussion of these short formularies in Louis Bouyer, *Eucharist: Theology and Spirituality of the Eucharistic Prayer*, trans. Charles Quinn (University of Notre Dame Press, Notre Dame-London, 1968), pp.55-58.

[3] See, for example, Schillebeeckx, *Jesus*, p.217.

[4] See, for example, the summary by Raymond Brown in 'The Resurrection in John 21— Missionary and Pastoral Directives for the Church' in *Worship* 64 (1990) 438-439.

[5] Acts of the Apostles, for example speaks of the movement 'from house to house' (8.3 and 20.20).

[6] For an overview of the table imagery and Jesus' table ministry in the New Testament, see Geoffrey Wainwright, *Eucharist and Eschatology* (Epworth Press, London, 1971), pp.25-42; a more focused introduction to food and meal in the Gospel of Luke is provided by Robert J. Karris in *Luke: Artist and Theologian* (Paulist Press, New York, 1985), pp.47-78.

Like Jesus, his first followers did not confine their prayer or table ministry to any single place or type of dwelling. The palatial homes of wealthy believers,[1] the more modest dwellings of poorer disciples,[2] ancient apartments,[3] public rooms[4] and hillsides provided the first followers of Jesus with the temporary settings they required for their gatherings. There the word was proclaimed, teaching imparted and healing offered. It was especially in such places that the members of this first community gathered for the breaking of the bread.

It seems that none of these places were permanent worship sites or used exclusively for cultic purposes. Rather, the followers of Jesus seemed to have moved and adapted their worship spaces according to need.[5] It is clear that whatever structure offered shelter to the early community was not considered the 'house of God'. Rather, the Christian community itself was the first and only *oikos tou Theou*.[6] The only true Christian architecture of the first century was one of living stones and not of brick or mortar. This community-centred ideal accompanied the development of Christianity from its rural Jewish origins into the urban Gentile mission.

THE FIRST CHRISTIAN 'MUSICIANS'

Any attempt to speak about 'musicians' in emerging Christianity is an exercise in anachronism. This is true, first of all, because of the previously noted auditory environment of New Testament Christianity which challenges and stretches our definition of 'music' and, by extension, 'musician'. It is also true because of the New Testament's silence not only about any 'musical' office, but also about virtually every cultic office. Although we know, for example, that the community gave thanks over bread and wine from the earliest times[7] we are never told who presided, or whether such presidency was continuously invested in one individual. Raymond Brown summarizes:

'The only thing of which we can be reasonably sure is that someone must have presided at the eucharistic meals, and that those who participated acknowledged his [sic] right to preside. How one got the right to preside and

---

[1] For example, the excavated villa at Anaploga, dated to the time of Paul, which Murphy-O'Connor believes is 'the sort of house in which Gaius acted as host to Paul and the whole church (Romans 16.23),' Jerome Murphy-O'Connor, 'The Corinth that Saint Paul Saw' in *Biblical Archaeologist* 47/3 (1984) 157.

[2] Thus Krautheimer interprets the phrase 'breaking bread from house to house' in Acts 2.42; see, Richard Krautheimer, *Early Christian and Byzantine Architecture*, 4th rev. ed., (The Pelican History of Art (Penguin books, London, 1986), p.24).

[3] See, for example, the illustrations in David Macaulay, *City: A Story of Roman Planning and Construction* (Houghton Mifflin Company, Boston, 1974), pp.71-75, 106-109.

[4] Referring to Acts 16.13 and 19.9, Krautheimer writes, 'Rarely would Christians be able to hire a public hall, as did the congregation at Ephesus at the time of St. Paul's visit,' (p.24).

[5] While it is true that residents of certain houses played key roles in the development of various local churches (for example, Prisca and Aquila, Acts 18.2-3 and 1 Cor. 1.16), one cannot conclude that such homes were permanent places for the emerging Christian cult.

[6] see Heb. 3.6; 1 Pet. 4.17; and 1 Tim. 3.15; also, *TDNT* 5:121.

[7] e.g. 1 Cor. 10.16-17; 11.23-24.

FIGURE 3. HOUSE AT POMPEII
Plan of the house of Pansa, Pompeii, second century BCE, after Helen Gardner, *Art through the Ages,* 8th rev. ed. by Horst de la Croix and Richard Tansey (Hartcourt, Brace, Jovanovich, San Diego, 1986), p.174.

whether it endured beyond a single instance we do not know; but a more plausible substitute for the chain theory is the thesis that sacramental "powers" were part of the mission of the church and that there were diverse ways in which the church designated individuals to exercise those powers—the essential element always being church or community consent (which was tantamount to ordination).'[1]

This phenomenon of a prayer-action led by an unspecified minister is the rule for the primitive Christian community. We know that some spoke in tongues (1 Cor. 14.2), some prophesied (1 Cor. 14.3), some interpreted (1 Cor. 14.5), some responded 'amen' to another's thanksgiving (1 Cor. 14.16), and some sang (Eph. 5.19) or read (Col. 4.16). No office is ever connected with these prayer-actions. We know that there were prayers, songs and readings, but we do not know who led them. This consistent lack of evidence, coupled with the previously discussed wide-ranging acquaintance of the primitive community with the *sheliach tsibbur* in synagogue worship, plus the very acceptance of such leadership by Jesus and Paul in the synagogue, suggests that volunteer prayer leadership continued in the emerging Christian cult.

Eric Werner contends that 'Jewish chant must have been transmitted to the Christian church mainly by cantors, to whom there are some epitaphs in the Roman catacombs'.[2] This hypothesis, though interesting, is nonetheless problematic for the New Testament period for a number of reasons. First and foremost, as previously demonstrated, there was no 'cantor', properly speaking, in the synagogues of the first century CE. Second, Werner's failure to identify the specific epitaphic evidence to support this contention makes it difficult to substantiate. Third, the epigraphic evidence that can be identified cannot be dated from the first century CE. Thus, while it is appropriate to acknowledge the influence of synagogue 'music' on that of emerging Christianity, it seems inappropriate to identify any permanent musician or 'cantor' as the ordinary transmitters of such influence.

EMERGING CHRISTIAN SONG
Establishing the kinds of texts that were 'sung' in the emerging Christian community is more complex than the same process for the synagogue or Temple of the first century CE. One practical reason for this added complexity is the existence of the New Testament, which provides us with an over-abundance of textual evidence for the new religion. A second reason is the unconventional nature of emerging Christianity which, while maintaining clear continuity with Judaism, was also in radical discontinuity with that tradition. Third, the extemporaneous nature of Jesus' own speech—which Amos Wilder characterized as dynamic, actual, immediate, and reckless of posterity[3] —as well as the corresponding revolution in the language of his disciples contributed to the evolution of new forms and a heightened proclivity for improvization in the New Testament period.

---

[1] Raymond Brown, *Priest and Bishop: Biblical Reflections* (Paulist Press, New York, 1970), pp.41-42.

[2] Werner, 'Jewish Music' in *NGDMM* 9:625.

[3] See the discussion of 'The Jesus Experience' above, in chapter one.

We will consider various types of texts under the headings of: short praise formulae, fragments and ejaculations, Infancy Canticles, God-hymns[1], Christological hymns[2], psalms, readings and table prayers.

Short Praise Formulae: Very often in early Christian writings one encounters short, standardized phrases praising God.[3] These *kurze Lobsprüche*, which appear to have developed from Jewish prayer forms, are generally called *berakoth* in Judaism.20 In Christian writings three types of short praise formulae are distinguishable by their respective *Grundwort:* doxology (*doxa*), eulogy (*eulogia*), and the thanks-formula (*charis*).

While there is common agreement that doxologies exist in the New Testament, there is little unanimity when it comes to defining the nature of a doxology. Some hold that some form of the word *doxa* or its equivalent is a defining element of all doxologies[4] while others do not.[5] Following Deichgräber, who designates doxology as any short *Lobsprüche* that agrees with the base form 'to (him) be glory for ever'[7], it is possible to identify twenty doxologies in the New Testament.[8]

The eulogy can be considered a *berakah* in the narrow sense of the word.[9] Like the doxology, this form first originated in Judaism and then was taken over and transformed by Christianity. The New Testament gives us seven *berakoth*.[10]

The thanks-formulae are those short phrases of thanksgiving found in the Pauline literature that follow the basic pattern of 1) a proclamation of thanks, 2) generally succeeded by the reasons for the thanks.[11] Such language, like that of

---

[1] The term 'hymn' is employed here with due caution. The next chapter will explore the various meanings and usages of this term. For now, it is sufficient to suggest that, in the present context, a hymn can be understood as any praise of God (or Christ) that employs what Kroll calls 'heightened speech'. See Josef Kroll, *Die Christliche Hymnodik bis zu Klemens von Alexandreia* (Königsberg im Br., 1921), p.11.

[2] These first four categories are borrowed from Reinhard Deichgräber, *Gotteshymnus und Christushymnus in der frühen Christenheit* (Vandenhoeck & Ruprecht, Göttingen, 1967).

[3] Kroll contends that praise and thanks, much more than intercession, characterize the enthusiastic and spontaneous prayers of emerging Christianity. Kroll, p.11.

[4] Deichgräber, p.24.

[5] Anton Baumstark, *Comparative Liturgy*, rev. ed. (Newman Press, Westminster MD, 1958), p.67.

[6] For example, Werner, *The Sacred Bridge* 1:274; also. A. Hamman in *Early Christian Prayers*, trans. Walter Mitchell (Longmans, Green, London, 1961), p.19.

[7] Deichgräber, p.25.

[8] Luke 2.14; Rom. 11.36, 16.27; Eph. 3.21; Phil. 4.20; Gal. 1.5; 1 Tim. 1.17, 6.16; 2 Tim. 4.18; 2 Cor. 11.31; Heb. 13.21; 1 Pet. 4.11, 5.11; 2 Pet. 3.18; Jude 25; Rev. 1.6, 5.13, 7.10, 7.12, 19.1. For a further discussion of these passages and their doxological character, see my 'The Question of Cultic Singing in the Christian Community of the First Century', unpublished M.A. Thesis (University of Notre Dame, 1980), pp.70-74.

[9] See Heinemann's discussion of *berakoth,* in *Prayer in the Talmud*, pp.77-103.

[10] Luke 1.68; Rom. 1.25, 9.5; 2 Cor. 1.3, 11.31; Eph. 1.3; 1 Pet. 1.3. For a further discussion of these New Testament *berakoth*, see my 'The Question of Cultic Singing', pp.74-77.

[11] Deichgräber, p.43.

the other short praise formulae, is characteristically emphatic and proclamatory. More so than the doxology or eulogy forms, the thanks-formula appears to be a mixture of Greek and Jewish elements and, uniquely Christian. There are at least six New Testament passages that can be considered thanks-formulae.[1]

Fragments and Ejaculations: The New Testament also contains what Ralph Martin calls 'Jewish-Christian fragments and ejaculations'.[2] These popular acclamations were naive expressions of belief,

'... untainted by theological arguments; the primitive Christian community had not yet established an organized worship. Its spontaneous acclamations represented the active part that the congregation played during the first two centuries, when no more than the core of the liturgy was in existence.'[3]

Klaus-Peter Jörns believes that such fragments are a key to understanding the interactive and 'responsorial' nature of early Christian worship.[4] There are at least five such fragments and/or ejaculations in the New Testament. They include *amen*, which concludes prayers and doxologies[5], prophecy, letters and writings.[6] The ejaculation *halleluia* appears to function as a doxology in the New Testament.[7] A third fragment is *hosanna*, that arises in the accounts of Jesus' triumphal entry into Jerusalem[8] where it appears to be a spontaneous acclamation.[9] *Marana tha*, which occurs only in 1 Cor. 16.22, is another fragment. Finally, the term *abba*—an Aramaic emphatic form of 'ab (father) that was used by Jesus 170 times in the Gospels[10]—seems to have been taken over very early into worship, possibly as a 'spirit-inspired cry'[11], as demonstrated by its usage in certain epistles.[12]

Infancy Canticles: In his study, *Birth of the Messiah*, Raymond Brown identified four Lukan passages as infancy canticles.[13] The first of these was the

---

[1] 1 Cor. 15.57; 2 Cor. 2.14, 8.16, 9.15; Rom. 6.17, 7:25; cf. 1 Tim. 1.12 and 1 Cor. 1.14 and 14.18.

[2] Ralph P. Martin, *Carmen Christi: Philippians 2.5-11 in Recent Interpretation and in the Setting of Early Christian Worship* (University Press, Cambridge, 1967), p.19.

[3] Werner, *The Sacred Bridge* 1:264.

[4] Klaus-Peter Jörns, 'Proclamation und Akklamation: Die antiphonische Grundordnung des frühchristlichen Gottesdienstes nach der Johannesoffenbarung' in *Liturgie und Dichtung* 1:187-208.

[5] Rom. 1.25, 9.5, 11.36, 16.27; Eph. 3.21; Gal. 1.5; Phil. 4.20; 1 Tim. 1.17, 6.16; 2 Tim. 4.18; Heb. 13.21; 1 Pet. 4.11, 5.11; 2 Pet. 3.18; Jude 25; Rev. 1.5-6, 7.10, 7.12, 19.1.

[6] Gal. 6.18, Rev. 1.7, and 22.20.

[7] Rev. 19.1-6.

[8] Mark 11.9-10; Matt. 21.9, 15; John 12.3.

[9] Eric Werner, 'Hosanna in the Gospels' in *Journal of Biblical Literature* 65 (1946) 103.

[10] Joachim Jeremias, *The Prayers of Jesus* (Fortress Press, Philadelphia, 1978), p.29.

[11] *Ibid*, p.34; also *TDNT* 1:6.

[12] Rom. 8.15 and Gal. 4.6; for a further discussion of all these fragments and ejaculations, see my 'The Question of Cultic Singing', pp.79-90.

[13] Raymond Brown, *The Birth of the Messiah* (Doubleday & Company, Garden City NY, 1977), p.346.

Magnificat (Luke 1.46-55), a 'cantena of Old Testament reminiscences'[1], not of Lukan origin, that was probably composed in a Jewish-Christian context.[2] Brown and others further intimate a liturgical usage of this hymn in the early community.[3] A second infancy canticle is the *Benedictus* (Luke 1.67-79). Like the *Magnificat*, the *Benedictus* was not a hymn of Lukan composition, but probably was a Jewish-Christian composition. The *Gloria in excelsis* (Luke 2.14), though numbered by some among the New Testament doxologies, also needs to be considered in the context of the other infancy canticles. Like the others, this canticle was probably a pre-Lukan composition that might have sprung from a community of Jewish-Christian *anawim*.[4] Drawing on a parallel that existed in the Qumran community, Brown comments that 'if the Qumran Anawim could compose hymns for the angels to sing, so could a Christian community of similar piety and liturgical interests.'[5] He even concedes that the *Gloria* and the parallel in Luke 19.38 'could constitute antiphonal responses'.[6] Finally, the *Nunc dimittis* (Luke 2.29-32) is another hymn that seems to have been composed by Jewish-Christian *anawim*.[7] The lyric character of the *Nunc dimittis*, like that of the other infancy canticles, suggest its cultic employment at an early stage in the development of Christian worship.

God-Hymns: A second category of larger hymnic forms in the New Testament is that of the God-hymn. These are distinguished from the short praise formulae by their length and are distinguished from the Christological hymns by their lack of any reference to Christ. Although there are only a few God-hymns that survive in the New Testament,[8] Deichgräber contends that this type of hymn played a significant role in emerging Christianity.[9] He bases this contention on the fact that many times the New Testament mentions that God is to be praised,[10] that there are many short praise formulae in the New Testament that could be remnants of larger pieces, and that Judaism—with its large number of

---

[1] Wilfred J. Harrington, *The Gospel According to St. Luke* (Newman Press, Westminster MD, 1967), p.53.

[2] Raymond Brown et al., *Mary in the New Testament* (Fortress Press, Philadelphia, 1978), p.140, n. 311.

[3] Brown, *The Birth of the Messiah*, p.354; also, see Douglas Jones, 'The Background and Character of the Lukan Psalms' in *Journal of Theological Studies* 19 (1968) 47.

[4] Brown, *The Birth of the Messiah*, p.427.

[5] *Ibid.*

[6] *Ibid.*

[7] *Ibid.*, p.350.

[8] Three occur as introductory eulogies at the beginning of epistles (Eph. 1.3-14; 1 Pet. 1.3-5; 2 Cor. 1.3-4), and a few other are simply two or three verse God-hymns (e.g. Rom. 11.33-36; 1 Tim. 6.15-16; Rev. 15.3-4).

[9] Deichgräber, p.60.

[10] e.g., Acts 2.47, 3.8, 10. 46; 11.18, 16.25, 21.20; 2 Cor. 9.13; Gal. 1.24; 1 Pet. 2.12; Jas. 3.9; ev. 15.6, 7. Gnilka concurs with this point, commenting on Eph. 5.19: 'To be sure, the thanks is ultimately directed to God, while the mediating place of Christ is clearly recognized'. Johannes Gnilka, 'Der Christushymnus der Philipperbriefes (2,6-11) und die neutestamentliche Hymnendichtung' in *Liturgie und Dichtung* 1.174.

hymns and hymn fragments—provided both the models and the impetus for the development of these larger hymnic forms.[1]

Christological Hymns: A final category of larger hymn types found in the New Testament is the Christological hymn. In offering his definition of a Christological hymn, Deichgräber emphasizes two elements: 1) the content of such a hymn is Christ and his work, and 2) the language, style and structure is clearly poetic.[2] Despite the ability to construct a definition or identify defining elements, here as with other lyric elements in the New Testament, there is no unanimity when it comes to designating Christological hymns or hymnic sections.[3]

This discrepancy in identifying hymns or hymn fragments or other lyric residue in the New Testament is magnified a hundredfold when one moves from the difficult task of identification to the perilous position of predicating a cultic usage of such elements. Thus the caution of Gerhard Delling is well remembered:

'Attempts have been made to identify various primitive Christian hymns or hymnal fragments in the New Testament. But such identifications must remain hypothetical, particularly as there is in the New Testament no attempt—and this is a pivotal point worth noting in itself—to use the Greek style of metrical hymns. The pieces in the New Testament which take the form of praise are in general so little controlled by any clearly discernible laws that for the most part judgment as to their character as hymns can claim only limited validity.'[4]

Such healthy scepticism is apparent in the many biblical scholars who are unwilling to accept the unchallenged attestations of their colleagues concerning hymnic materials in the New Testament. Many are the commentators who disagree that hymnic elements exist, or who ignore the question altogether. Yet, even Delling for all his caution, admits to 'many hymn-like passages in primitive Christian liturgy', recognizes that 'it is possible that improvised songs were sung in the service', and affirms that some New Testament passages (e.g., 1 Tim. 3.16) are plainly 'old hymns'.[5]

It is not possible to affirm that all of the short praise formulae, fragments and ejaculations, infancy canticles, God-hymns and Christological hymns outlined above were employed in ancient Christian worship, or would have been recognizable as 'musical' elements when they were. Yet, given what we know

---

[1] For an extended discussion of the various God-hymns in the New Testament, see my 'The Question of Cultic Singing' pp.99-112.

[2] Deichgräber, p.106.

[3] Deichgräber designates Phil. 2.6-11; 1 Tim. 3.16; Heb. 1.3; 1 Pet. 2.21-24; and Col. 1.15-20 (pp.118-154). Martin, in *Carmen Christi*, lists Heb. 1.3, Col. 1.15-20; 1 Tim. 3.16; John 1.1-14; 1 Pet. 1.18-21, 2.21-25, 3.18-21, and Phil. 2.6-11 (p.19). Jack Sanders, in his *The New Testament Christological Hymns* (University Press, Cambridge, 1971), suggests Phil. 2.6-11; Col. 1.15-20; Eph. 2.14-16; 1 Tim. 3.16; 1 Pet. 3.18-22; Heb. 1.3; and John 1.1-14 (p.vii).

[4] *TDNT* 8:500.

[5] Gerhard Delling, *Worship in the New Testament*, trans. Percy Scott (Westminster Press, Philadelphia, 1962), pp.82, 87 and 88 respectively.

about the auditory environment of first century CE Palestine, the many lyric elements of Jewish worship, the influence of Jewish worship on the followers of Jesus, the explosion of newly composed psalms and hymns in various segments of first century CE Judaism such as the community at Qumran[1], the ecstatic nature of the Christian kerygma, as well as the multiple New Testament passages that have been identified at one time or another as lyric, hymnic or song-like[2], it is very probable that these or similar texts did punctuate the emerging Christian cult and could be considered 'musical' elements of that cult in the broad sense of that term. This leads us to agree with Joseph Gelineau that there must have been 'an intense lyrical quality in the life of the Apostolic church.'[3]

Psalms: We have already illustrated the tenuous role that psalmody played in synagogue worship at the dawn of Christianity. In our previous discussion we concluded that, while the spirit of prayer embodied in the psalms may have influenced synagogal prayer in the first century CE, it is questionable whether psalms were commonly sung in first century synagogue worship.

While there is more basis for giving some role to sung psalmody in emerging Christian worship, its place in that cult is yet quite ambiguous. Such ambiguity stems from the fact that the psalms are, on the one hand, the Old Testament book most frequently cited in the New Testament[4] yet, on the other hand, their presence in Christian worship is not explicitly noted before the end of the second century CE.[5]

---

[1] Paul Bradshaw, *Daily Prayer in the Early Church* (Oxford University Press, New York, 1982), p.21.

[2] The literature here is vast; apart from those sources already mentioned, a further sampling of opinions is found in: Rudolf Bultmann, 'Bekenntnis und Liedfragmente im ersten Petrusbrief' in *Exegetica* (1967) 285-297; Elizabeth Schüssler Fiorenza, 'Wisdom Mythology and the Christological Hymns of the New Testament' in *Aspects of Wisdom in Judaism and Early Christianity*, ed. Robert Wilken (University of Notre Dame Press, Notre Dame, 1975), pp.17-41; Joachim Gnilka, 'Der Christushymnus der Philipperbriefes (2,6-11) und die neutestamentliche Hymnendichtung' in *Liturgie und Dichtung*, 1:173-185; Robert Gundry, 'The Form, Meaning and Background of the hymn quoted in 1 Tim. 3.16' in *Apostolic History and the Gospel*, Festschrift für F. F. Bruce (Paternoster, Exeter, 1970), pp.203-222; F. Manns, 'Un hymne judéo-chrétien: Philippiens 2, 6-11' in *Euntes Docete* 29 (1976) 259-290; J. M. Robinson, 'Die Hodajot-Formel in Gebet und Hymnus des Frühchristentums' in *Apophoreta. Festschrift für Ernst Haenchen*, eds. Walther Eltester and Franz Heinrich Kettler (Topelmann, Berlin, 1964), pp.194-235; and G. Wilhelmi, 'Der Versöhnen-Hymnus in Eph. 2.14ff' in *Zeitschrift für neutestamentliche Wissenschaft* 78 (1987) 145-152.

[3] Joseph Gelineau, 'Music and Singing in the Liturgy' in *The Study of Liturgy*, ed. Cheslyn Jones et al., (Oxford University Press, New York, 1978), p.444.

[4] The single such text that is cited the most in the New Testament is Ps 110. See Gerhard Dautzenberg, 'Psalm 110 im Neuen Testament' in *Liturgie und Dichtung*, 1:141.

[5] In the apocryphal *Acts of Paul* (ca. 190 CE) there is a reference to the 'singing of David's psalms and hymns' (*Acta Pauli*, ed. and trans. Wilhelm Schubart and Carl Schmidt (J. J. Augustin, Hamburg, 1936), pp.50 and 51, line 11). The references to 'psalms, hymns and spiritual songs' in Eph. 5.19 and Col. 3.16, while tantalizing in their reference to 'psalms', offer no precise distinction between these three genres, and offer no proof that the Davidic psalms were used in early Christian worship. cf. *TDNT* 1:164.

As in the synagogues of the era, it is possible that the psalms served as a book of readings for the early Christian community.[1] It is also possible that the psalms—some of which were traditional for home rituals like the passover[2]—found a place in the new home rituals of the followers of Jesus. The 'passover memory' that shaped emerging Christian table practice[3] could have contributed to this development. What was probably more determinative for the adoption of psalmody in this early period, however, was the previously noted revolutionary style of Jesus' preaching that evoked a similar revolution in the language of his disciples. If the preaching of the early community had more in common with town criers or auctioneers than traditionally understood rabbinic discourse and if, as Dodd contends, Jesus was revealed through oral tradition and charismatic experience[4], then it would not be surprising that, in this heightened auditory environment, the new followers of the way sought poetic expression for their faith. Fragments from the psalms might have found their way into preaching or proclamation, new psalm-like compositions emerged, and traditional biblical psalms were reinterpreted in light of the Jesus experience. Given the wide diversity of first century CE practice, however, it would be hazardous to suggest that there was any set pattern for employing psalms within Christian worship.

Readings: There are numerous New Testament indicators that reading quickly developed as a statutory element in early Christian worship. For example, the well known precedent from the Jewish synagogues of the day found no rejection in the New Testament, which remembered Jesus taking a central role in the proclamation of the word.[5] Certain passages, like the story of the two disciples on the road to Emmaus[6], suggest a word and table sequence that is an unquestionable pattern of Christian worship by the second century.[7] Furthermore, the New Testament explicitly mentions public reading a number of times.[8] Such references are related to New Testament evidence that the 'Word of God' is understood not only as the Old Testament[9], but also as the word of

---

[1] Thus Bradshaw, for example, suggests that the 'use of the Psalter may possibly have been in the formal services of the word and alongside non-canonical compositions at the *agape*' (Bradshaw, *Daily Prayer*, p.45); also, Joseph Gelineau, 'Les psaumes a l'époque patristique' in *La Maison-Dieu* 135 (1978) 101.

[2] see Mark 14.26 and Matt. 26.30; Joachim Jeremias, and others, accept this as a reference to the singing of the second half of the passover *Hallel* (Pss. 114 or 115 to 118). See his *Eucharistic Words of Jesus*, p.55.

[3] See, for example, Thomas Talley, *The Origins of the Liturgical Year* (Pueblo Books, Collegeville, 1986), pp.3-5.

[4] See the discussion of 'The Jesus Experience' above, in chapter one.

[5] Luke 4.16-21.

[6] Luke 24.13-35.

[7] Justin Martyr, *First Apology* 67.3-8.

[8] For example, there is reference to the public reading of letters in the congregation (2 Thess. 5.27; Col. 4.16), the cultic reading of the Old Testament (Luke 4.16; Acts 13.27, 15.21; 2 Cor. 3.15; Rev. 1.3).

[9] Frederick Crowe, *Theology of the Christian Word* (Paulist Press, New York, 1978), p.25.

Jesus[1], as Jesus himself[2], and even the word about Jesus.[3] This expanded understanding of the Word of God suggests what might have been 'read'[4] in the gatherings of the primitive community, i.e. sections from the Old Testament, sayings or stories of or about Jesus as they took written form, and various pastoral letters, like those of Paul. Maybe most telling for the emergence of this statutory element is the rise of the written Gospel itself.

Table Prayers: A final genre of texts that served the rising lyricism of the Christian community were the table prayers that accompanied their emerging eucharistic practice. For a pious Jew, no meal experience could begin without the breaking of bread and an accompanying *berakah.*[5] On Sabbaths and festivals this pre-meal blessing found a post-meal complement in the extended blessing known as the *birkat hamazzon.*[6] These traditions were well known to the Jewish followers of Jesus who borrowed them and adapted them.[7] Although the meal proper eventually separated from this ritual in the Christian community[8], the prayers remained and evolved into what we know as eucharistic prayers.

'SONG' FORMS

In our discussion of Jewish precedents, we noted that there is more surety about ancient Jewish prayer forms than there is about their melodic or rhythmic structure. A similar remark could be made about ancient Christian 'song'. Consequently, we will concentrate more on the forms of the 'music', and offer an occasional reflection about melodic or rhythmic elements.

Short Praise Formulae: These brief forms often have the character of a conclusion. It is possible that, for example, the doxology originally served as a response to a preaching event and passed into the Christian assemblies and

---

[1] *TDNT* 3:1107.

[2] 'The NT goes even farther than the Old in what it makes of the Word . . . As is the case of no other religion, the Word is here the proper name of a person, the Son of God.' (*TDNT* 3:1117).

[3] Crowe, pp.22-42; Kittel concludes that since the word about Jesus is identical with Jesus himself, then what is said about Jesus can be said about the gospel: it is truth (2 Cor. 4.2), a reliable word (1 Tim. 1.15), and a two-edge sword (Heb. 4.12), that demands a response and effects the promised salvation (*TDNT* 4:117).

[4] Public 'reading', as it developed in the early community, may not always have been an exact parallel to modern practice, especially in reference to the use of a book or written text. While there is great precedent for the use of scrolls, letters and other written forms in the early Christian community, it is also possible—given the role of memory in this heightened auditory environment—that public 'reading', for example, consisted of a recitation of the sayings or parables of Jesus. This could have been especially true in that period before such sayings were codified in written or Gospel form.

[5] See *Berakoth* 6:1-8.

[6] The classic study is by Louis Finkelstein, 'The Birkat Hamazzon' in *Jewish Quarterly Review* 19 (1928-29) 211-263.

[7] See, for example, Thomas Talley, 'From *Berakah* to *Eucharistia*: A Reopening Question' in *Worship* 50 (1976) 115-137; *idem*, 'The Literary Structure of Eucharistic Prayer' in *Worship* 58 (1984) 404-420.

[8] 1 Cor. 11 already attests to this process.

organized worship.[1] There is a strong link between the doxology and the 'amen': of the twenty doxologies we identified in the New Testament, only three do not have an 'amen' at their conclusion.[2] Two of the eulogies we identified in the New Testament also function as a concluding pattern and are wed to the 'amen'.[3] Although none of the 'thanks-formulae' we identified are followed by 'amen' in the text, some do function as concluding formularies,[4] and could have been sealed by 'amen'. This hypothesis is supported not only by the emphatic and spontaneous nature of these formulae, but also by the tantalizing reference in 1 Corinthians 14.16 in which Paul urges the community to prayer in such a way so that others can comprehend and 'say "amen" to your thanksgiving'. Delling summarizes about the liturgical usage of the doxology—a summary applicable to all of these formulae:

> 'The usage was ... not invented, presumably, in the letter writing of the primitive church, but was imported from elsewhere. And the most obvious place of origin is in worship: for rounding off teaching, exhortation and prepared discourses, an expression of praise was most suitable. It gave the congregation the opportunity to make the message its own, to acknowledge it as binding by its amen.'[5]

As to the musical quality of these short formulae, they are better understood as joyous outbursts and spontaneous acclamations than sustained musical events. These are more liturgical 'shouts' than 'songs'.

Fragments and Ejaculations: Even more than the short praise formulae did the fragments and ejaculations enumerated above serve as spontaneous acclamations in the emerging worship of the early Christian community. Their brevity and emphatic quality suggests a heightened unpredictability about their usage. It is true that, as previously noted, the 'amen' often served to conclude the prayer or preaching of another and—at least in the synagogues of the time—was an essential sign of the congregation's involvement in the worship.[6] The 'amen' was, undoubtedly, a key response in emerging Christian worship as well.[7] There is also evidence that the 'halleluia' served as a concluding response, both in

---

[1] Beda Rigaux, *The Letters of St. Paul*, ed. and trans. Stephen Yonick (Franciscan Herald Press, Chicago, 1968), p.132.

[2] Luke 2.14; 2 Cor. 11.31; Rev. 19.1.

[3] Rom. 1.25, 9.5.

[4] e.g. Rom. 7.25 and 2 Cor. 9.15.

[5] Delling, *Worship in the New Testament*, p.64.

[6] The congregational role was so important in the synagogue that the story is often recounted of the synagogue in Alexandria, where the size of the gathering made it difficult for the congregation to know when a benediction had ended. Thus, an official of the synagogue stood on the platform in the centre of the synagogue and waved a handkerchief as a signal for the people to say their 'amen'. (B. *Sukkah* 51b).

[7] See, for example, Fitzmeyer, 'Pauline Theology' in *NJBC* 82:16.

Judaism[1], and early Christianity.[2] It is also possible that 'hosanna', which apparently served as a congregational response in the primitive community[3], sometimes served as a concluding acclamation. Yet more than predictable cultic rejoinders to well known cues, these are textual remnants of the spontaneous cries that punctuated the rites of the nascent Christian community.

Infancy Canticles, God-Hymns and Christological Hymns: It is not possible to demonstrate, beyond a reasonable doubt, that all of these larger 'hymn' forms—or even that any of them—found an enduring place in emerging Christian worship.[4] What seems clear, however, is that such larger hymnic forms—similar to those that do survive in the various strata of the New Testament—were characteristic of the evolving cult. The very survival of so many larger hymnic remnants in the New Testament seems incontestable evidence for this assertion.

As to how such hymns were performed, or what they sounded like, one can only guess. The presumed presence of volunteer prayer leaders—Christian counterparts to the *sheliach tsibbur*—suggests that some of these larger forms may have been improvised by a leader, with the assembly repeating each line in turn.[5] It is even more probable that—given the length of some of these texts as well as the fluid state of their content in the oral mode—such hymns were performed by a volunteer prayer leader while the assembly may have added some phrases of blessing or affirmation at least at the end of the prayer.[6] It is also conceivable that some of these hymns were performed as solos, without congregational response. The caution with this last suggestion, however, is eloquently offered by Paul himself, who counsels the Corinthian community to seek only those gifts that build up the community. He continues,

'I will pray with the spirit and I will pray with the mind also; I will sing with the spirit and I will sing with the mind also. Otherwise, if you bless with the spirit, how can any one in the position of an outsider say the "amen" to your thanksgiving when he does not know what you are saying' (1 Cor. 14.15-16).

---

[1] The congregation responded with 'halleluia' after each sentence of the Hallel psalms according to Heinemann (*Prayer in the Talmud*, p.145) and others.

[2] 'Halleluia' appears to function as a doxology in its only New Testament occurrence (Rev. 19.1-6), as well as in the extra-biblical *Odes of Solomon*, in which 'halleluia' concludes every ode. See *The Odes of Solomon*, ed. and trans. James H. Charlesworth (University of Montana Press, Missoula MT: 1977). Charlesworth suggests that the Odes are of Jewish Christian origins, dating from very early; other scholars (e.g. W. Bauer, *NTA* 2:809) believe their time of composition to be comparable to that of the book of Revelation or latter.

[3] for example, in Didache 10.6.

[4] For a survey of opinions for and against the liturgical usage of each of the Infancy Canticles, God-Hymns and Christological Hymns noted above, see my 'The Question of Cultic Singing', pp.90-122.

[5] Such was how the *shema* may have been performed in some synagogues at the time of Jesus.

[6] As previously noted, this is one accepted hypothesis for the performance of the *amidah* in the synagogues.

Paul's admonition suggests that—while there were, undoubtedly, situations in which individuals gave singular voice to hymns in communal worship—it is improbable that such singular hymnody was emblematic of the evolving cult. Even more unlikely was the ability of any soloist to suppress the community's affirmation of such spirited praise.[1]

Attempting to establish the melodic or rhythmic contour of these larger forms is virtually impossible. However, Avenary's suggestion of 'prayer modes'—plastic enough to fit such fluid prose texts[2]—offers one possible model for conceiving how such hymns may have been performed.[3]

Psalms: The previously noted ambiguity concerning the place of psalms in emerging Christian worship makes suggesting anything about their performance a relatively precarious enterprise. If the psalms continued to function as a book of readings for the early Christian community, then the performance style would be similar to other cultic readings.[4] If the psalms found a place in the new home rituals of the followers of Jesus it is probably that their form dictated the style of their performance: some could have been led by an individual with others joining on a refrain after each colon; others could have employed a responsorial form in which the congregation responded to each verse with some brief refrain; the assembly might have punctuated other psalms with cries of 'halleluia'; it is even possible that some texts were rendered strophically.[5] As to the musical nature of such forms, no one is sure.[6] Idelsohn and his disciples would like to suggest that musical forms yet extant in the 19th and early 20th

---

[1] Jörns stresses that hearing or listening were never ends in themselves in early Christian worship, but had the purpose of calling forth the 'amen' of the community, which was the true aim and symbol of the Spirit at work in the community. Jörns, 'Proclamation und Akklamation', 1:193.

[2] Avenary, 'Music' in *EJ* 12:578.

[3] Commenting about Phil. 2.6-12, Werner notes: 'Another important factor in the formation and expansion of early Christian music was its Gentile wing, which brought the Palestinian-Syrian tradition into close contact with the Hellenized world. According to some scholars, the passage Phil. 2.6-12 might perhaps be understood as a free poetic outburst. If their view is correct, we must consider it the first perceptible deviation from the spirit and structure of Hebrew poetry. There is no parallelism, not even a trace of lines similar to each other in length or in the number of accentuated syllables. If such a piece was ever sung, which is doubtful, it could not have been performed in the manner of traditional Jewish psalmody or like a canticle' (Werner, 'Music' in *IDB* 3:467).

[4] These will be considered in the following section.

[5] For a further discussion of these forms, see our discussion of 'psalmody' in the previous chapter.

[6] Avenary believes that a style of performing the psalms that can safely be ascribed to the first centuries CE entails 'the sung recitation ... generally on a single pitch, with melodic figures (cadences) attached to the middle and the end of the verse. Verses usually begin with an intonation motif. This modest configuration is repeated through the entire psalm; thus the music does not distract the listener's attention from the text.' (Avenary, 'Jewish Music', 1:955).

centuries are suggestive of sounds from the dawn of Christianity.[1] It is an interesting, even credible, but nonetheless unprovable hypothesis.

Readings: As we have already noted, readings from various sections of the Hebrew scriptures were rendered by different musical modes or formulae in the ancient synagogue.[2] Whatever modes were in existence at the rise of Christianity were probably borrowed by the followers of Jesus—especially the Jewish Christians—in the cultic proclamation of the Hebrew scriptures. When Gentile communities began the cultic proclamation of readings from the Hebrew Scriptures it is probable that they borrowed at least the idea if not the melodic and rhythmic structure of the Hebrew modes for cantillation. This suggestion finds support in the fact that there appear to be no other models outside of Judaism in the ancient world for such cantillation.[3] As to the 'musical' settings for the other elements that were 'read', one may suggest that—borrowing Eric Werner's categories[4]—such public proclamations migrated from ecphonesis (or a semi-musical recitative) to cantillation (regular musical chant) the more clearly such proclamations were identified as the 'word of the Lord'. Given that Christianity gave birth to new genres of God's word—the Gospels and Epistles—so too did they eventually develop distinctive musical formulae that were related to but different from their Jewish predecessors.[5] Such was especially true as the Gentile community came to prominence in the new religion.[6]

---

[1] See his *Hebräisch-orientalischer Melodienschatz*; a sampling of these examples can be found in Idelsohn, *Jewish Music in its Historical Development*, pp.62-64; also, Ergon Wellesz, *A History of Byzantine Music and Hymnography*, 2nd ed. (Clarendon Press, Oxford, 1961), pp.35-37.

[2] While probably not all these modes existed in the earliest stages of synagogue development, Idelsohn notes the eventual emergence of the following: the Pentateuch mode, the mode of Ruth, special modes for poetical portions of the Pentateuch, the Prophetic mode, the mode of Lamentations, the mode of Job, various modes for the Psalms, and the mode of Esther. For a further discussion of these various modes as well as musical illustrations, see Idelsohn, *Jewish Music*, pp.39-66.

[3] 'Psalmody and melodic reading are common traits of all the "peoples of the bible." Repeated attempts to find an archetype of it in pagan antiquity have not succeeded.' (Avenary, 'Music' in *EJ* 12:578).

[4] 'plain recitation (spoken), ecphonesis (*Sprechgesang*, or a semi-musical recitative) and cantillation (regular musical chant).' (Werner, *Sacred Bridge*, 1:104).

[5] Thus Werner concludes, 'It is not possible to compare simply Jewish and Christian practices concerning the chant of the lesson. Here the respective traditions are too incommensurate: while Judaism has established a minutely elaborated system of ecphonetic accents applied to every word, the Churches have limited themselves mostly to closing or pausal accents of verses.' (*Sacred Bridge* 1:456).

[6] See Eric Werner's comments on the musical influence of the 'Gentile wing' in the formation and expansion of early Christian music, above. One caution in attempting to assess the influence of the various musical traditions of Gentile believers on emerging Christian worship is that Judaism at the time of Jesus was already a Hellenized Judaism, clearly influenced by Greek culture [see, for example, Martin Hengel, *Judaism and Hellenism: Studies in their Encounter in Palestine during the Early Hellenistic Period*, trans. John Bowden (Fortress Press, Philadelphia, 1975); also, *idem., The 'Hellenization' of Judaea in the First Century after Christ*, trans. John Bowden (SCM Press, London, 1989)]. The growing dominance of Gentile Christians, however, must have significantly magnified such Hellenizing influences.

Borrowed Spaces and Emerging Christianity [the first century CE] 65

Table Prayers: Just as a Jew could not simply speak a public reading or declaim a public prayer without some level of musicality, so it was not possible for them to enact the rituals surrounding their meals without 'music'. The context of these meal prayers[1] as well as their structure suggest that such prayers were lead by a single individual, with responses from the assembled family.[2] The followers of Jesus adopted and adapted this practice, retaining much of the structure and content, but interpreting it in view of the Jesus experience[3], something that Jesus himself probably did at the Last Supper. Even when the meal proper was separated from the prayer the same performance practice seems to have endured. In attempting to discover what such prayers might have sounded like, we again have recourse to the previously discussed 'prayer modes', that would have been flexible enough to fit such fluid prose texts.[4]

INSTRUMENTS

We have already noted how instrumental music—apart from the shofar —never found a place in synagogue worship. Thus the precedent for, what in another age would be called 'a cappella' worship, did not originate with the followers of Jesus, but with the rabbis who effectively prohibited the use of all instrumental music from Jewish worship until the nineteenth century. It was this spirit that permeated emerging Christian worship from its inception.

While there are many references to instruments in the New Testament[5], such references—aside from some in Revelation—never mention instruments in terms of the emerging Christian cult. Even though Quasten[6] and other writers from earlier in the church accept the references in Revelation as proof that instruments were employed in the first century cult, contemporary scriptural scholarship calls for a more symbolic interpretation of these passages.

The reasons for the absence of instrumental music—probably even the *shofar*—from Christian worship are complex. Almost all would agree that one contributing element is a consistent affirmation of the primacy of vocal music in emerging Christianity. It is the word-event, the parable, the kerygma that is central—to such an extent that even the meal could be spiritualized without anything essential being lost. In such a context, instrumental music would not play a critical role. Some have also suggested that another reason for the absence of instrumental music in the New Testament cult was a conscious rejection of this

---

[1] that is, in the setting of an extended family where there was a natural and ordinary leader: the head of the household.

[2] What existed was not so much a text as a formula that was improvised by the head of the household in three stanzas or on three separate themes: each of which was probably concluded with a doxology-type refrain by the gathered family.

[3] See Talley, 'From Berakah to Eucharistia' especially pp.89-92.

[4] Avenary, 'Music' in *EJ* 12:578.

[5] e.g. cymbals (1 Cor. 13.1), gongs (1 Cor. 13.1), pipes (Matt. 9.23; 11.17; Luke 7.32; 1 Cor. 14.7; Rev. 18.22), trumpets (1 Cor. 14.8), shofars (Rev. 8.2, 6, 12; 9.1-13), harps (Rev. 5.8; 14.2; 15.2).

[6] Johannes Quasten, *Music and Worship in Pagan and Christian Antiquity*, trans. Boniface Ramsey (Pastoral Press, Washington DC, 1983 [1973]), pp.72-73.

music. Thus Werner, commenting on 1 Corinthians 13, writes:

'Explicitly stated here is the primacy of vocal performance over any instrumental music. Implicit is the contempt of all instrumental music, and the emphatic disparagement of "gong" and "cymbals", two of the Temple's percussion instruments . . . In general Paul considers all musical instruments lifeless or soulless (1 Cor. 14.7).'[1]

James McKinnon would appear to disagree with this perspective, suggesting that 'a doctrine of opposition to instruments' in the Christian community did not develop until the third and fourth centuries. To the contrary, Christian music was so exclusively vocal in its early stages that the occasion to criticize the use of instruments in church never arose.[2] McKinnon, however, probably overstates his case.

While it is true that, as McKinnon notes, early Christianity was in continuity with the synagogue service, he fails to acknowledge that the synagogue and the Temple were complementary elements in first century Judaism. Emerging Christianity had a much more tenuous relationship to the Temple which, although never completely rejected, was a place of increasing tension for the disciples. Furthermore, Temple sacrifice, which was essential to Jewish cult, became increasingly peripheral for emerging Christianity, especially with the mission to the gentiles. Thus, I would suggest that there was an element of 'rejection' in Christianity's earliest assessment of instrumental music: a rejection wed to a growing rejection of the type of priesthood, cult, and religious view embodied in the Temple.

Eric Werner draws a corollary between sacrifice, hierarchy and art music, on the one hand, and *logos* worship, rudimentary democracy and folk-song on the other.[3] Instrumental music more clearly allies with the former, and 'a cappella' music with the latter. The absence of instrumental music in the primitive Christian community, therefore, is not simply because they had no other option. Rather, it seems intimately wed to the embrace of democratic forms of worship, a rejection of Temple priesthood and sacrifice, and to the process of spiritualization[4] that marks the emerging cult.

SUMMARY ON 'CHRISTIAN MUSIC' OF THE FIRST CENTURY CE

In discussing the evolving cult of the early Christian community, Thomas Talley once remarked that early Christian practice reflects patterns which are as meticulously different from, as they are broadly grounded on, Jewish tradition. Talley's observation is useful when attempting to summarize Christian music of the first century CE. There is, for example, much continuity in terms of texts,

---

[1] Werner, 'Music' in *IDB* 3:466.
[2] James McKinnon, *Current Musicology* 1 (1985) 74-75; McKinnon spins out his complete argument in 'The Church Fathers and Musical Instruments' (Ph.D. Dissertation, Columbia University, 1962).
[3] *Sacred Bridge* 2:149-175.
[4] e.g. the spiritualization of the Temple sacrifice, the spiritualization of the meal, etc.; see Finkelstein's discussion of such spiritualization in terms of the Didache, ('The Birkat Hamazzon', p.214).

musical forms, styles of 'musical' leadership and melodic build blocks—especially between Jewish synagogue, home rituals and emerging Christian cult. Many of the texts that were part of the lyrical horizon of early Christian worship (like the Infancy Canticles) were borrowed from Judaism, the practice of publicly cantillating readings is distinctively Jewish, and even the priority of vocal music to the exclusion of instruments was a synagogal innovation. Yet, the tonal landscape of early Christianity cannot be understood simply in terms of continuity with Jewish synagogal or domestic worship. Texts were borrowed and adapted, the nature of public reading was redefined in terms of gospel and epistle, and the traditional patterns of Jewish chants—already under the influence of Hellenism—were increasingly influenced by the musical traditions of Gentile believers.[1]

Maybe more significant than any of these for emerging Christian song was the previously stressed ecstatic nature of this new kerygma and cult. Taking its cue from the speech of Jesus that appears to have been radically different from that of other Jewish teachers of the time, we noted the extemporaneous, improvisatory and dynamic nature of the early Christian kerygma. Thus spontaneity and immediacy of expression were hallmarks of the early kerygma and, by extension, early worship. Therefore, while maintaining a certain continuity with synagogal and domestic Jewish precedents, Christian cult was nonetheless something revolutionary and distinctively charismatic. This suggests an intense lyricism in early Christian worship, which prized responsorial forms[2], punctuated as it was by shouts, acclamations, hymns, improvised chants, and even the gift of tongues.[3]

---

[1] 'Since the early Christians improvised much of their chant, it is possible to postulate the influence of the folk music of the Hellenized Syrian littoral (i.e. music neither learned nor popular; the music of the taverns and markets). Modern religious music suggests this by analogy.' (Hannick, 'Christian Music' in *NGDMM* 4:365).

[2] See Jörns, 'Proklamation und Akklamation' *passim.*

[3] i.e. 'glossolalia', mentioned in 1 Cor. 14, which is quite different from the foreign languages of Acts 2.4-11. See the discussion in Jerome Murphy-O'Connor's commentary on 'The First Letter to the Corinthians' in *NJBC* 49:63-64; also, Behm's article on 'glossa' in *TDNT* 1:722-726.

5. The Era of The House Church [The Second and Third Centuries CE]

THE SETTING

What is notable in the era of the house church is not that Christians gathered in domestic dwellings—for that was something they did from the inception of the Jesus movement. What is notable in this era is that eventually specific houses were acquired and set aside for cultic use. At the beginning of the movement, borrowed rooms and the homes of believers were important gathering places for the fledgling community. With the destruction of the Temple and the separation of the Christian community from the synagogue, these domestic settings became virtually the only place for community worship.[1]

It is difficult to generalize about the types of homes that existed in the Roman empire during the first centuries of the common era.[2] It was not uncommon to find large, four-sided structures for the wealthy, in the urban centres of the empire. The normal inclusion of a large dining room well suited for eucharist as well as a pool in the atrium adaptable for baptism made them very serviceable buildings. Structurally these houses faced inward with the open spaces at the centre of the building. The resulting walled off interior provided shelter from the commotion of the street and the disapproving gaze of pagan neighbors and authorities.[3]

Homes for the lower or middle class were quite different. In the Eastern provinces, according to Krautheimer, there existed single family dwellings of up to four storeys high. The only large room was the dining room on the top floor, that often opened on to a terrace. Krautheimer imagines that it was such a dwelling, with the congregation crowded into the upper room, that served as the setting for the incident at Troas during which a young man—apparently dozing on the window-sill—fell to the ground and was raised from the dead by Paul (Acts 20.7-12).[4] In Rome, tenement houses with horizontal apartments were the rule. Some of these apartments may not have included a dining room, so the community used any available room of appropriate size for their gatherings.[5]

---

[1] Exceptions to this can be found, for example, in the apocryphal *Acts of Paul* 11.

[2] As L. Michael White notes, 'House patternings varied considerably across the empire: the Italian villa, the Greek peristyle, the Hellenistic-oriental multistoried *insula*, apartments, and others had their own local stylistic traditions. We must expect, then, that ... there was considerable diversity from place to place depending on the local circumstances of each cell group' (White, *Building God's House in the Roman World*, p.107).

[3] Macauley provides a splendid introduction to such homes, *City: The Story of Roman Planning and Construction*, pp.66-70; for a more scholarly introduction, see, Alexander McKay, *Houses, Villas and Palaces in the Roman World* (Cornell University Press, Ithaca NY, 1975).

[4] Krautheimer, p.24.

[5] *Ibid.*

Krautheimer believes that before 200 CE, Christian congregations were restricted to these 'inconspicuous dwellings of the lower class'.[1] Murphy-O'Connor, on the other hand, suggests that even from the first century, the Christian community gathered (although not exclusively) in the homes of wealthy believers[2]—the precedent for which can be found in the ministry of Jesus himself.[3]

In the early history of these domestic gatherings one can imagine the worshipping community respecting the limitations of another family's dwelling. Permanent changes in the structure would have been inappropriate. The community likely rearranged furniture in order to accommodate its worship. In the dining room, or some other large gathering space, a single table could have been used for eucharist with a chair for the host or bishop who led the worship. As the size of the community increased and the limits of ordinary rooms were tested it is possible that a community looked for larger homes in which to gather.

Eventually communities sought permanent homes for worship and other gatherings. It is impossible to say for certain when this first occurred. As previously noted, Krautheimer suggests that prior to the year 200 CE Christian congregations were 'limited to the realm of domestic architecture, and further, to inconspicuous dwellings of the lower class.'[4] It is generally true that homes provided the setting for Christian worship until the dawn of the 4th century CE. If, however, Krautheimer means to suggest that prior to the year 200 CE Christians did not own any domestic buildings or set such buildings aside exclusively for ecclesial use, his hypothesis can be argued only from silence.

The clearest ancient archaeological evidence of a Christian 'house-church' is that of Dura-Europos.[5] Destroyed in 257, the building dates from around 230, and seems to have been structurally altered to suit the needs of the Christian community, which was in possession of the structure, between 240 and 250.[6]

---

[1] *Ibid.*, also n. 24, p.456; the reasoning outlined in the latter is faulty, for it presumes that, for example, gardens and audience halls could not have been used by the early Christian community because they would have been 'utterly unsuitable for the ritual meals of the believers'. What Krautheimer fails to note, however, is that the meal is one of the first elements to drop out of the emerging Christian cult, and Paul in his First Letter to the Corinthians already announces its absence.

[2] Jerome Murphy-O'Connor, 'The Corinth that Saint Paul Saw', p.157; *idem, St. Paul's Corinth: Texts and Archaeology* (Michael Glazier, Wilmington DE, 1983), pp.153-161.

[3] for example, the Lukan account of Jesus dining with Simon the Pharisee (7.39-50), Zaccheus the chief tax-collector (19.1-10), and Mark's account of Jesus entering the house of Jairus, the synagogue official (Mark 5.35-43).

[4] Krautheimer, p.24 and n. 24, p.456.

[5] The literature on this excavation is vast. For an introduction to the church, see Krautheimer, p.27; for a more general introduction to the excavation, see Clark Hopkins, *The Discovery of Dura-Europos* (Yale University Press, New Haven, 1979); the classic study on the church is C. H. Kraeling, *The Christian Building: The Excavations At Dura Europos conducted by Yale University and the French Academy of Inscriptions and Letters: Final Report* 8/2 (Yale University Press, New Haven, 1967).

[6] Krautheimer, p.27. On the issue of adaptation or renovation as a transitional stage of early Christian architecture, see White, *Building God's House in the Roman World*, pp.21-22.

FIGURE 4—HOUSE CHURCH AT DURA EUROPOS
Plan of the house church at Dura Europos after Peter Cobb, 'The Architectural
Setting of the Liturgy' in *The Study of the Liturgy*, ed. Cheslyn Jones *et. al.* (Oxford
University Press, New York, 1978), p.481.

Literary evidence from various other places of the time confirm that other communities also had their own buildings.[1]

The reasons why Christians found it important or even necessary to establish permanent settings for their gatherings, are multiple and complex. Contributing factors included the rapid growth of the Christian community[2], the increased complexification of the cult with commensurate demands upon the worship space[3] and wide spread toleration of Christians in and outside of the empire.[4] White believes that one can document the emergence of a more distinctively Christian material culture between the time of Justin Martyr (d. ca. 165) and the *Constitutio Antoniana* (212), which conferred citizenship upon all free inhabitants of the empire.[5] These and other factors testify to Christianity's transition from the status of sect and movement to a full-scale religion.

Beyond these measurable characteristics, Kelber's reflections on the rise of the written gospel might offer a further insight into why permanent domestic churches developed within Christianity. Kelber suggests that the development of the written gospel within the Christian community must not be seen as a natural, evolutionary progression from oral to written forms but as a radical alternative.[6] Oral forms, in Kelber's view, support images of the heroic and dynamic, whereas written forms give people the distance necessary to reassess and more completely to appreciate the experience of the heroic. In specific reference to the Jesus experience, Kelber summarizes, 'It may thus not be an exaggeration to claim that it was with Mark's extraordinary narrative that Christian consciousness was jolted out of oral infancy and partial amnesia of Jesus' death toward a fully historicized grasp of the life and death of the messiah.'[7]

Could not something similar be said of permanent ecclesial settings *vis-à-vis* borrowed spaces in early Christianity? The former may not have been so much a natural evolution from the latter, but a counterreform. The growth in the number of believers, their increased visibility and acceptance, their gradual

---

[1] The Emperor Severus Augustus (d. 235), for example, allowed the Christians to purchase a public property. *The Writers of Augustan History: Severus Alexander* 49.6.

[2] According to Harnack, for example, there could have been as many as 50,000 Christians in Rome by 250 (Adolph von Harnack, *The Mission and Expansion of Christianity in the first Three Centuries*, trans. James Moffatt, 2nd rev. ed. (Williams and Norgate, London, 1908), p.247).

[3] The *Didascalia Apostolorum* (early third century), for example, offers a relatively detailed instruction for the physical disposition of the community during worship (12).

[4] Persecutions of Christians were usually short-lived and confined to specific locations: for example, under Nero (d. 68 CE) in Rome, Domitian (d. ca. 96) in Rome, Trajan (d. 117) in Asia Minor, Marcus Aurelius (d. 180) in Lyons, and Decius (d. 251) and Diocletian (d. 305) throughout the empire.

[5] White, p.118; in support of this claim he cites Graydon Snyder who considers the period between 180 and 200 as the time during which 'Christian art, funerary symbolism, and the building began to achieve their own cultural definition.' (*ANTE PACEM: Archaeological Evidence of Church Life Before Constantine* (Macon GA, 1985), pp.163-165, as cited in White, p.118).

[6] Kelber, p.209.

[7] Kelber, p.211.

abandonment of itinerant leadership and growing reliance on resident episcopoi[1] and their image of themselves—not so much as sect or even local religion, but as a belief-system and church that spanned the empire—called forth a radically different setting for their cult. In some respects, like the rise of the written gospel, the emergence of the permanent house church marked the end of an heroic era and enabled the community to move toward a fully historicized grasp of the life and death of the messiah.

EMERGING CHRISTIAN 'MUSICIANS'

Unlike the previous era, this period does offer ample witness to the singing of the Davidic psalms in various Christian gatherings. What this period does not yield, however, is any evidence of a psalmist, cantor or any other that might be considered a permanent or official musician in the Christian community.

This is somewhat striking since literary sources from the period testify to the existence of numerous other liturgical ministers and officials. Hippolytus (d. ca. 236), for example, notes that there were deacons, subdeacons and readers[2]; Cornelius of Rome (d. 253) in his letter of 251 to Fabius attests to the presence of acolytes, exorcists and doorkeepers[3]; the *Didascalia* (ca. 225) knows of deaconesses[4]; and Tertullian (d. ca. 225) considers widows to be part of the clergy.[5] Yet, in none of these listings, church orders or correspondence do we hear of a singer, psalmist or cantor.[6]

One exception could be an epitaph from Hadrian in Bithynia which Leclercq claims is 'certainly anterior to the peace of the Church, probably appearing in the second or third century.'[7] The epitaph commemorates an eighteen-year-old man who was known for 'chanting the praises of the most high, and training all the faithful to chant the sacred psalms and the reading of the holy books.'[8] If this epitaph originated in the second or third century it could be our earliest known reference to someone leading the assembly in psalm singing. Leclercq's contention that this young cantor held the office of *psaltes* and *anagnostes*[9], however, is overdrawn. The epitaph speaks of no office but only of action, not of a 'chanter' but of 'chanting'. Furthermore, the epitaph attests to the intimate relationship between singing and reading, between psalms and lections—and not, as Leclercq

---

[1] See, for example, Nathan Mitchell, *Mission and Ministry*, Message of the Sacraments 6 (Michael Glazier, Wilmington DE, 1982), especially pp.137-200.

[2] *Apostolic Tradition* 4.

[3] This letter is recorded in Eusebius' *Ecclesiastical History* 6.43.

[4] *Didascalia* 2.26.6.

[5] *On Monogamy* 11.1.

[6] For a survey of the documentary evidence for singers in the early church, see Brian Joseph Sparksman, 'The Minister of Music in the Western Church: A Canonical-Historical Survey' (Unpublished JCD dissertation (Catholic University of America, 1980), especially the first two chapters).

[7] H. Leclercq, 'Chantres' in *Dictionnaire d'Archéologie Chrétienne et de Liturgie* 3 (1914) 345.

[8] *Ibid.*

[9] *Ibid.*

suggests—because in this era there were 'not always sufficient hierarchical personnel to fulfil the diverse functions of the church'.[1] Rather, it was because the community as yet saw little distinction between the sung and the publicly spoken. As such a division between singers and speakers, or between cantors and readers, was unnecessary at that time, so 'reader' was the only designation given to those responsible for the cantillated, be that psalms or lessons.[2]

CHRISTIAN 'SONG'

During this period the previously discussed forms from the New Testament, readings and anaphora continued to exist as lyrical elements of the worship. Since these would have functioned virtually the same as in the previous era, we will not give them specific attention here. Rather, we will focus on the psalms of David, 'hymnodic psalmody' and metrical hymns.

Psalms: Prior to the third century of the common era there is little explicit evidence that the Davidic psalms were anything like a 'songbook' for the early Christian community. This led some, like Balthasar Fischer, to suggest that the Old Testament psalms were never a part of Christian cult during the first two centuries.[3] Fischer argues that the early Church only turned to the psalter as a songbook in response to the questionable hymn texts that were 'radically compromised by gnostic abuses'. He concludes that the trend toward accepting the psalter in Christian worship occurs only around the year 200 CE.

It is true that, along with the previously noted apocryphal *Acts of Paul*, the earliest clear evidence for psalms in Christian worship clusters around the year 200 CE.[4] Evidence before this time is fragmentary and ambiguous. As previously noted, it is possible that the psalms served as a book of readings for the early Christian community[5]; that psalm fragments might have found their way into preaching or proclamation; that new psalm-like compositions emerged; and that traditional biblical psalms were reinterpreted in light of the Jesus experience. It is not possible, however, to ascertain any set pattern for employing psalms within Christian worship of the first century. What is new in the third century, therefore, is not so much that psalms are employed for the first time in Christian worship, but that patterns for their usage develop and clarify. Tertullian, for example, indicates that psalm-singing is an ordinary element of the 'liturgy of the word' for the Sunday assembly.[6]

---

[1] *Ibid.*

[2] *Apostolic Constitutions* (ca. 380 CE) seems to be breaking new ground when it indicates that someone besides the reader of the lessons should sing the psalms, 2.57.6.

[3] 'Le Christ dans les psaumes' in *La Maison-Dieu* 27 (1951) 86-113.

[4] for example, possibly Clement of Alexandria's (d. 215) *Stromata* 7.7.49; Hippolytus' *Apostolic Tradition* ch. 25 (ca. 215 CE); the *Didascalia Apostolorum* (ca. 225 CE) 6.5; Tertullian's *On the Flesh of Christ* 20.3.

[5] That the book of Psalms continued to be considered a prophetic book and, therefore, possibly read as such in early Christian worship is supported, for example, by the writings of Justin Martyr (d. ca. 165) who quotes from the psalms in his discussion of the Hebrew prophets who foretold the coming of Christ, as e.g., in *Apology* 1.31-41.

[6] 'the Scriptures are read, psalms are sung, sermons are delivered and petitions are offered' (*On the Soul* 9); for a general discussion of the role of psalmody in the liturgy as reflected in the writings of Tertullian, see E. Dekkers, *Tertullianus en de geschiedenis der Liturgie* (Desclée de Brouwer, Brussels-Amsterdam, 1947), pp.31-36.

As to why psalmody became a constitutive element of Christian worship after the third century, one can only surmise. Fischer's suggestion that the biblical psalms were an appropriate and effective 'antidote' to more contemporary compositions of questionable content certainly could have been one reason. Another is what Eric Werner characterizes as a trend from spontaneous to more organized patterns of prayer.[1] It is around the year 200, for example that the New Testament canon began to be defined[2] and the first written model for a eucharistic prayer appeared.[3] This general move toward standardization in creedal and prayer formulae could have been the impetus for the further standardization of Christian worship. The adoption of the Davidic psalms was one more step in this process.

Hymnodic Psalmody: We have already employed the term 'hymn' as a designation for certain larger lyrical forms in the New Testament such as God-hymns and Christological hymns.[4] Such works were largely 'poetical-prose'[5] compositions of uneven metre and stress[6] constructed in imitation of biblical patterns like the Davidic psalms.[7] Cattin and others call such works 'hymnodic psalmody'[8] to distinguish them from the metrical and strophic structures that are to arise later. It is possible that this is the lyric genre which lies behind Pliny's

---

[1] Werner, 'Music' in *IDB* 3:467.

[2] 'In the East Clement of Alexandria and in the West Tertullian were developing the basic language of the two Testaments. In the same general period, the Muratorian Fragment and Origen gave lists of NT books—a sign that the concept of a collection of Christian Scriptures had taken hold.' (*NJBC* 66:81).

[3] Hippolytus, *Apostolic Tradition* 4.

[4] In attempting to discern what might be considered an early Christian hymn, Ralph Martin offers the following direction: 'There are no metrical standards available at this point in the development of Christian worship. Metrical verses came later; and it is only in the third century that we have examples of anapaestic metre and musical notation. The criteria which are available are stylistic tests, of which the most obvious traits are: a certain rhythmical lilt ascertainable when the passage is read aloud, a correspondence between words and phrases which are placed in the sentences in an obviously carefully selected position, not always *ad sensum*; the use of *parallelismus membrorum* (i.e. an arrangement into couplets); and traces of a rudimentary metre and the employment of rhetorical devices such as *homoeoteleuton*, alliteration, antithesis and *chiasmus*.' (*Carmen Christi*, pp.12-13).

[5] a term of Egon Wellesz that respects the fact that these are 'poetic' works that have a strong affinity with prose forms, (*A History of Byzantine Music and Hymnography*, p.149). The border between prose and poetry was often blurred in 'hymns' from the classical world at time time as well, e.g. those of Pliny the Elder (d. 79 CE), and Apuleius (d. ca. 123 CE). (Wünsch, 'Hymos' in *Paulys Real-Encylopädie der classischen Altertums Wissenschaft*, ed. Wilhelm Kroll (J. B. Metzler, Stuttgart, 1914) IX/1:180).

[6] Anton Baumstark calls these 'prose hymns', ('Hymns (Greek Christian)' in *Encyclopaedia of Religion and Ethics*, ed. James Hastings (Scribner's Sons, New York, 1915) 7:5 and *passim*).

[7] For a further description of the structure of Hebrew psalmody, see Corbin, p.132.

[8] Cattin, *Music of the Middles Ages I*, p.18; Kroll uses the term 'prose-hymn' [*Prosahymnus*], p.8.

allusive reference to believers chanting[1] 'a hymn to Christ as to a God' in his letter to Trajan in ca. 112 CE.[2]

One extant collection of Christian hymnodic psalmody is the *Odes of Solomon*. This collection of 42 odes was probably the work of Jewish Christians in Palestine in the late first century CE.[3] Written in imitation of the Davidic psalms, these *psalmi idiotici* employ a characteristic parallel structure in which each verse is divided in half (a colon) by a caesura (or sentence-stop)[4]—a Semiticism captured in Charlesworth's translation of Ode 1:

1. The Lord is on my head like a crown,
   And I shall never be without him.
2. Plaited for me is the crown of truth
   And it caused Thy branches to blossom in me.
3. For it is not like a parched crown that blossoms not;
4. But thou livest upon my head,
   And have blossomed upon me.
5. Thy fruits are full and complete;
   They are full of Thy salvation.

Other hymnodic psalms can be found in such apocryphal acts as those of John[5] and Thomas.[6] According to Wellesz, although these works are transmitted in Greek, the language demonstrates many characteristics of Semitic poetry.[7] The works of certain gnostic writers can also be considered hymnodic psalms.[8] Important here is Bar-Daisan (d. 222) who, with his son Harmonius, composed a

---

[1] *'carmen dicere'* may mean to 'sing' or 'chant' a hymn: a reading enhanced by Tertullian's *Apology* 2.6, which quotes this passage from Pliny, and 'definitely understands *carmen dicere* in the sense of *canere'* (Willi Rordorf, *Sunday*, trans. A. K. Graham (SCM Press, Ltd, London, 1968), p.259, n. 3).

[2] *'carmen Christo quasi deo dicere secum invicem'* (Pliny, *Letter* 10.96); see Ralph Martin, 'A Footnote to Pliny's Account of Christian Worship' in *Vox Evangelica III*, ed. Ralph Martin (Epworth Press, London, 1964), pp.51-57; a more recent survey of opinion on this passage can be found in Jorg Christian Salzmann, 'Pliny (*Ep.* 10.96) and Christian Liturgy—a Reconsideration' in *Studia Patristica* 20 (1989) 389-95.

[3] *The Odes of Solomon*, ed. and trans. James Charlesworth (Scholars Press, Missoula MT, 1977), pp.90, 113 and *passim*.

[4] 'The biblical [poetic] line consists of two balanced cola. The balance between them can be metrical (the roughly equal length of the cola), syntactic, morphological, phonic, semantic, and of other types too disparate to catalogue here. Every line has approximate metrical balance. In all of the other areas the balance can run from nothing or next, to nothing, to moderate to extreme. . . This balance between the cola can be and is called parallelism.' (Aloysius Fitzgerald, 'Hebrew Poetry' in *NJBC*, 12:11.

[5] for example, the 'Hymn to Christ', translated in *NTA* 2:228-232.

[6] for example, the 'Psalm of Thomas', translated in *NTA* 2:498-504.

[7] Wellesz, *A History of Byzantine Music and Hymnography*, p.149.

[8] For example, the Ophite hymn (Origen, *Against Celsus* 6.31; Hippolytus, *Refutation of all Heresies* 5.9.8), the Naassenians' psalm (Hippolytus, *ibid.* 5.10.2), the Valentinus psalm (Hippolytus, *ibid.* 6.37.6-8), and the hymn of Basileides (Clement of Alexandria, *Stromata* 6.12.81-8).

new psalter.[1] As for orthodox writers, Kroll would argue for the existence of 'hymns' in the works of Ignatius of Antioch (d. ca. 107) and Melito of Sardes (d. ca. 190).[2]

A further stage in the evolution of this genre is evident in the third century hymn *Phos Hilaron*. No longer a binary structure of parallel half-verses with a break in the middle, this Greek text is composed of three strophes, each of which contains four lines.[3] Despite this structural development, *Phos Hilaron* must still be considered a piece of 'poetical-prose'[4], as it lacks the alternation of long and short syllables as well as the regular distribution of stresses that characterizes classical poetry and will characterize later Christian hymnody. This is true of a number of other Greek poetical-prose compositions from the early Christian centuries.[5]

At the beginning of the third century Tertullian noted the existence of hymnody among the heretics. Fontaine believes this to be an important reference, bolstering the hypothesis that heretics were the first to employ 'hymns' on a regular basis.[6] Tertullian's information about worship in his own community[7] suggests that, in Africa at the beginning of the third century, there existed charismatic hymnody, individually improvised and yet demonstrating a certain concurrence between biblical canticles and the new improvizations.[8] The continuity between these forms, and the possible reliance of new improvizations upon biblical prototypes suggests, again, that the type of hymnody under discussion is really hymnodic psalmody.

Metrical Hymnody: While Judaism provided the models for the development of hymnodic psalmody in emerging Christianity, it was the classical poetry of the Greco-Roman world that provided models for the emergence of metrical hymnody. Here the central organizing principle was meter which, although present in biblical poetry and later works written in imitation of biblical poetry, was not the basic organizing principle of biblical verse or its literary offspring.[9]

---

[1] Only a single quotation from this psalter is preserved in the works of Ephraem the Syrian, *Works* 2:483; the historian Sozomen (early fifth century) reports that Harmonius was accomplished in Greek learning, and 'was the first to subdue his native language to metres and musical laws' (*Church History* 3.16).

[2] i.e. Ignatius' *Letter to Polycarp* (3.2), and fragment 13 from Melito's writings; (Kroll, pp.19-22).

[3] See, E. R. Smothers, 'Phos Hilaron' in *Recherches des science religieuse* 19 (1929) 266-283.

[4] Wellesz, *A History of Byzantine Music and Hymnography*, p.149.

[5] Baumstark enumerates some of these in 'Hymns (Greek Christian)' pp.5-6.

[6] Jacques Fontaine, 'Les Origines de l'hymnodie chrétienne latine' in *La Maison-Dieu* 161 (1985) 42.

[7] 'After water for washing the hands and lamps have been brought in, each is invited to take the floor and sing to God according to his own ability, either drawing upon the scriptures or improvising something of his own.' (*Apology* 39).

[8] Fontaine, p.149.

[9] The exact role and nature of metre in biblical poetry continues to be a widely debated question. See Fitzgerald, *NJBC* 12:16-20.

Christians' acquaintance with classical poetry may be detectable as early as Paul who, in his discourse to the Athenians (Acts 17.16ff), seems to refer to two poetic Greek texts: the *Phaenomena* of Aratus of Soli (d. ca. 239 BCE), and the *Hymn to Zeus* by Cleanthes (d. ca. 232 BCE).[1] This acquaintance did not translate into early acceptance. The first extant example of an orthodox Christian hymn composed in classical metre is the 65 short line, anapaest (– – /) work of Clement of Alexandria (d. 215).[2] It is quite probable that Clement was imitating a style of metrical poetry that was adopted earlier by gnostic believers.[3] Wellesz contends that such hymns 'represent an attempt by education men to preserve Greek civilization', and that Clement's hymn of praise to Christ 'shows how the master of the Catechetical school tried to combine the spirit of Greek poetry with Christian theology.'[4] A few lines from Clement's hymn make the point:

'King of Saints, Almighty Word
of the Father, Highest Lord,

Wisdom's head and chief
Assuagement of all grief;

Lord of all time and space
Jesus, Saviour of our Race.'[5]

There is considerable disagreement as to whether or not this hymn was ever employed in worship.[6] Apart from its usage, this work of Clement of Alexander does attest to the emergence of a style of Christian hymnody that is not exclusively or essentially dependent upon Semitic prototypes, but finds its roots in classical Greek forms. From this experiment will develop works most accurately described as Christian hymns, i.e., new works of metrical[7] poetry, in which the texts come to be structured into stanzas of two or more lines, with each stanza employing the same metre, and same number of lines.

---

[1] Fontaine, pp.34-35.

[2] *Paidagogos* 3.101.3; for an analysis of the structure of the hymn, see Gerhard May, 'Der Christushymnus des Clemens von Alexandrien' in *Liturgie und Dichtung* I:260-265.

[3] Baumstark, 'Hymns' p.6. Also, see B. Herzhoff, 'Zwei gnostische Psalmen. Interpretation und Untersuchung von Hippolytus, *Refutatio* V.10.2 und VI.37.7' (Unpublished doctoral dissertation (Bonn, 1973)).

[4] Wellesz, *A History of Byzantine Music and Hymnography*, p.149; this opinion is complemented by that of Bruno Stäblein who believes that Clement was the first Christian to consider carefully the nature of both pagan and Christian music in his time. ('Frühchristliche Musik' in *Musik in Geschichte und Gegenwart*, ed. F. Blume, 4:1038).

[5] *Clement of Alexandria*, ed. by Alexander Roberts and James Donaldson, Hymns trans. by W. L. Alexander, Ante-Nicene Fathers 2 (Charles Scribner's Sons, New York, 1926), p.296.

[6] Kroll, for example, thinks that the hymn had nothing to do with worship (p.12), whereas Quasten thinks it 'perhaps to represent the official prayer of praise of the School of Alexandria' (Johannes Quasten, *Patrology*, 3 vols. (Utrecht-Antwerp, 1950-1960), 2.11).

[7] It is the metrical construction which, according to Kroll, is the 'formal criterion' for defining a hymn in Christian worship' (Kroll, p.8.).

Clement's testimony in the East has some parallels in the West. Fontaine suggests that, little by little in the West, there is a 'thaw' in Christianity's opposition toward pagan poetry, beginning in the third century.[1] The progressive openness to traditional pagan poetry is evident in the *Octavius* of Minucius Felix (d. ca. 220 CE), where there is great reverence for the work and 'theology' of Virgil, as well as in the work of Arnobius (d. ca. 330) and his pupil Lactantius (d. ca. 320). At the same time, Christian leaders became increasingly critical of pagan music practices. As McKinnon summarizes,

'The first hint of the polemic against pagan music appeared in the work of the late second-century converted rhetorician Tatian, who wrote: "I do not wish to gape at many singers, nor do I care to look benignly upon a man who is nodding and motioning in an unnatural way." The polemic grew in explicitness and intensity throughout the third century, particularly with Latin Africans like Tertullian and Arnobius, and became a commonplace among the major figures of the fourth like John Chrysostom, Ambrose and Augustine.'[2]

Thus at the same time that there is growing critique of pagan musical practices, there is increased toleration and adaptation of pagan forms by Christian poets. This paradoxical confluence of adaptation and critique contributed to the first golden age of Christian hymnody, represented by Hilary of Poitiers (d. 367) and Ambrose (d. 397) in the West, and Ephraem the Syrian (d. 373) in the East.

The Oxyrhynchus Hymn: Along with all of the literary, epigraphic and iconographic monuments to Christian music in the first three centuries, there is one musical fragment that survives from this formative period of Christianity. The Oxyrhynchus hymn takes its name from Oxyrhynchus (Bahnasa), an archaeological site in Egypt[3] where many thousands of Greek, Latin, Coptic and Arabic documents were discovered between 1897 and 1907.[4] Papyrus 1786 in this collection contains the closing words and music of a hymn to the Trinity[5]

---

[1] Fontaine, p.42; what follows draws upon Fontaine's summary.

[2] He continues, 'Why the polemic should have been absent from the writings of early church fathers and so prominent in those of later ones is not easy to explain... Perhaps it was due to cultural factors... the attitude of the primitive church might be characterized by simplicity and directness. The later fathers on the other hand, all thoroughly educated in the classical tradition, might be said to have shared the musical puritanism of pagan intellectuals, taking it—for reasons of their own—beyond all precedent... Quasten... sees the principal motivation of the patristic polemic as the close association of pagan musical practice with the "pagan cult of idols".' (McKinnon, pp.2-3).

[3] In central Egypt, about 200 kilometres south of Cairo, and 15 west of the Nile.

[4] The fruit of these excavations, led by R. P. Grenfell and A. S. Hunt, they have been edited as *The Oxyrhynchus Papyrus*, 55 vols. (Egypt Exploration Society, London, 1898-1988).

[5] Wellesz's translation reads, 'while we hymn Father and Son and Holy Spirit let all creation sing amen, amen, amen, Praise, Power... to the one Giver of all good things, amen, amen' (Egon Wellesz, 'Early Christian Music' in *Early Medieval Music up to 1300*, New Oxford History of Music, vol. 2, ed. Anselm Hughes (Oxford U.P., London, 1955), p.4). It is possible that this is not a hymn to the Trinity, but simply a Trinitarian doxology, concluding a hymn that could have had another textual focus.

dating from the end of the third century.[1] The text is in Greek and notated in what is sometimes called classical Greek vocal notation. While there is much unanimity when it comes to transcribing the hymn[2], which many agree to have been based on a diatonic Hypolydian scale, there is much disagreement concerning the relationship of the hymn to classical Greek music[3], and the proper manner for performing the hymn.[4] One further wonders to what extent this singular monumental—which may or may not have been employed in worship—is typical of Christian music at any stage of its development.

'SONG FORMS'

Apart from the Oxyrhynchus fragment, none of the monuments of Christian music in this era provide sufficient information to allow for the melodic reconstruction of early Christian music. Consequently, in this section we will concentrate more on the forms of the music, and offer an occasional reflection about melodic or rhythmic elements. Since this has already been done above for the Oxyrhynchus hymn, this hymn will not be treated separately below.

Psalms: The increased information about the employment of the Davidic psalms in this period allows more clarity as to the performance of these psalms in the Christian cult. Tertullian, for example, notes that when Christians gather for common prayer, 'The more diligent in prayer are accustomed to add in their prayers the "hallelujah" and such kind of psalms at the close of which the company may respond.[5] This reference suggests that the community knew responsorial forms in which 'alleluia or some other responsory as part of the text itself ... were chosen so that the company could respond at the end of the verses.'[6] Evidence for responding to psalms with 'alleluia,' already evident in Jewish practice, is clear in the second and third century of the Christian era.[7]

---

[1] The original publication of the hymn is to be found in *The Oxyrhynchus Papyri* 15 (1922) 21-25. The literature on this musical fragment is vast; for an introduction to it, see Quasten, *Music and Worship in Pagan and Christian Antiquity*, p.105, n. 59b; a few additional references can be found in Hannick, Christ Church, NGDMM 4:371.

[2] Compare the six transcriptions by various scholars in Stäblein, 'Frühchristliche Musik', 4:1053-1056.

[3] See the useful summary of opinions in Quasten, *Music and Worship in Pagan and Christian Antiquity*, p.105, n. 59b.

[4] 'The conclusion of this hymn gives no indication of a congregational refrain, and some think that it was meant to be sung by a soloist,' (Hannick, p.367); Quasten, on the other hand, thinks this hymn to be a witness to the *una voces dicentes* of the early Christian community, (*Music and Worship*, pp.70-71).

[5] *Concerning Prayer* 27.17.

[6] Robert Taft, *The Liturgy of the Hours in East and West* (Liturgical Press, Collegeville, 1986), p.18.

[7] For example, the *Odes of Solomon* employ 'alleluia' at the close of all but the first two of its forty-two odes; Hippolytus also acknowledges the practice of reciting 'alleluia psalms', to which people respond with 'alleluia' (*Apostolic Tradition* 25). Victor Saxer believes that this form was instrumental in the development of responsorial chant in Christian worship. See Victor Saxer, *Vie liturgique et quotidienne Carthage vers le milieu du IIIe siècle*, Studi di Antichità Cristiana 29 (Pontificio di Archeologia Cristiana, Vatican, 1969), p.220.

Evidence that the community responded to a psalms with more than a single word is sketchy in this period. An examination of the literature has led Caglio to conclude that responsorial psalmody did not exist in the East much before the end of the third century[1] and that Ambrose introduced it into the West, in imitation of the Eastern practice.[2] Such a conclusion, however, seems to draw too sharp a distinction between responsorial forms that employed only a single word (e.g. 'Alleluia') and those that employed phrases, half verses or full verses as the response. Furthermore, as Cattin suggests 'the global scale of subsequent developments is such that the argument [against the existence of the responsorial psalm before the third century] *e silentio* seems very weak, the more so because the Biblical precedents for psalms with a refrain are particularly notable . . . even if their plan is not exactly that of the Christian responsorial psalm.'[3]

Besides these responsorial variations[4], it is also probable that this epoch knew both solo psalmody as well as unison performance of psalms. Evidence for the former can be found in the following passage from Tertullian's writings: 'each is asked to step forward and sing, according to his ability, a hymn to God, either from the Holy Scriptures or his own composition.'[5] Although 'hymn . . . from the Holy Scriptures' could refer to some non-psalmic song from the Hebrew Bible or a New Testament canticle, it is also quite probable that Tertullian is referring to psalm singing here, especially given the other notable references to psalm-singing in Tertullian's works. Evidence for unison congregational psalm-singing is rooted in the patristic notion of 'singing with one voice'.[6] Ignatius of Antioch (d. 107) is often cited as the classical patristic source for such thinking.[7] Clement

---

[1] He suggests the first incontestable evidence is found in the work of Athanasius (d. 373), *Defence of his flight* 24. Athanasius' language suggests that this responsorial practice is somewhat older, though Caglio would not want to push it much earlier than the end of the third century (E. T. Moneta Caglio, *Lo Jubilus e le origini della salmodia responsoriale*, Jucunda Laudatio 14-15 (1976-1977), pp.58-59).

[2] *ibid.*, pp.5-30.

[3] Cattin, p.10; also, Helmut Leeb who, reiterating the stance of Jungmann, holds that responsorial psalm singing was the only form of psalm singing known to the Church until the middle of the fourth century. (*Die Psalmodie bei Ambrosius*, Wiener Beiträge zur Theologie 18 (Herder, Wien, 1967), p.17).

[4] Avenary distinguishes seven types of responsorial structures: 1) repetition of every phrase or verse by the choir; 2) intonation by the precentor; 3) a 'motto' from the first verse recurs as refrain; 4) 'halleluia' as responsorial call; 5) alternate singing of hemistichs; 6) repetition of verses; and, 7) additions to the text of psalms. Avenary, 'Formal Structure of Psalms and Canticles', pp.3-6.

[5] *Apology* 39.18; further citations can be found in Caglio, p.51, n. 90.

[6] For a more thorough discussion of this concept, see Quasten, *Music and Worship in Pagan and Christian Antiquity*, pp.66-72.

[7] 'therefore it is fitting that you should live in harmony with the will of the bishop, as indeed you do. For your justly famous presbytery, worthy of God, is attuned to the bishops as the strings to a harp. therefore, by your concord and harmonious love Jesus Christ is being sung. Now do each of you join in this choir, that being harmoniously in concord you may receive the key of God in unison and sing with one voice through Jesus Christ to the Father'. (*Letter to Ephesians* 4:1-2, trans. by Kirsopp Lake, from *Apostolic Fathers*, 2 vols., Loeb Classical Library (Harvard University Press, Cambridge MA, 1912; rpnt. 1959) I:177).

of Alexandria specifically speaks of psalm singing in this mode: 'It is fitting to bless the Maker of all things before we partake of food; so, too, at a feast, when we enjoy his created gifts, it is only right that we sing psalms to him. In fact, a psalm sung in unison is a blessing, and it is an act of self-restraint.'[1] There appears to be no evidence from this period for alternating or antiphonal psalmody.[2]

Hymnodic Psalmody: The wide range of forms that emerged in imitation of Davidic psalmody called forth an equally wide range of performance styles. The *Odes of Solomon*, for example, with their recurring 'alleluia' refrain suggest a performance style akin to the alleluiac psalms, in which the assembly punctuated a solo performance with 'alleluia' or some other such refrain.[3] A previously cited reference from Tertullian[4] attests to the existence of solo (improvised) *psalmi idiotici* in the early patristic period. Finally, the strophic construction of a prose hymn such as *Phos Hilaron*, suggests that the Christian community of this era also had in their repertoire prose compositions that were performed in unison by a group or the entire assembly. While there is less explicit evidence to prove that hymnodic psalmody of the early Christian community was performed responsorially, the previously postulated ubiquitous nature of this form in emerging Christianity makes it difficult to refute out of hand its employment with hymnodic psalms.[5]

As to the sound of such performances, one can only hypothesize. It is probable that hymnodic psalmody more closely allied with Davidic psalmody relied on similar music.[6] The emergence of new hybrids, like *Phos Hilaron*, undoubtedly stretched the musical vocabulary of the early Christian community.[7]

Metrical Hymnody: A central characteristic of emerging Christian metrical hymnody is a text of metrical poetry, structured into stanzas of two or more lines, with each stanza employing the same metre, and number of lines. Such hymns could have been performed by soloists or even small groups.[8] It is also possible that they were performed responsorially, wherein the leader sang each line, and the assembly repeated it. The repetition of poetic and melodic units, characteristic of this structure, also suggests that such hymns were sung by an assembly without any division in the text. The common singing of hymns by the whole

---

[1] *Paidagogos* 2.44, trans. Simon P. Wood, *Christ the Educator*, The Fathers of the Church 23 (Fathers of the Church, Inc., New York, 1954), pp.132-3.

[2] Although alternating and antiphonal are sometimes considered synonymous, antiphonal has many other meanings. See, for example, Bernard Botte, 'Antiphona' in *Sacris Erudiri* 4 (1952) 239-244.

[3] In the 'Hymn of Christ' found in the apocryphal *Acts of John*, for example, 'amen' is a continuing response. See *NTA* 2:228-232.

[4] *Apology* 39.18.

[5] The psalter of Bar-Daisan and his son Harmonius, for example, could have presumed such performance.

[6] See the discussion of 'Song Forms (Psalmody)', above in chapter 4.

[7] Fontaine suggests that the music for *Phos Hilaron* must have been 'melodic and accentual' (p.41).

[8] There is evidence, for example, that the heretical bishop Paul of Samosata (third century) had 'choirs' of women singing 'hymns' in worship. See the report in Eusebius, *The History of the Church* 7.30.10.

assembly could also be suggested by the previously noted concern for 'singing with one voice' as well as the universal tradition, in the ancient Greek-speaking world, for choruses singing in unison.[1]

Attempting to imagine the sound of such hymns is difficult. Hannick's summary is clear and typical: 'Although the texts of some Christian hymns are known, their melodic structure is not. Even the Oxyrhynchus fragment containing musical notation ... cannot serve as a basis for investigation, and the evidence of the Fathers is inconclusive.'[2] One tantalizing but inconclusive piece of evidence from the Fathers is the complaint Clement of Alexandria registers against the use of chromaticisms.[3]

INSTRUMENTS

The previous summary on the use and place of instruments in the emerging Christian cult corresponds to this period as well. Although the literature expands, and references to musical instruments abound[4], instruments still played no significant role in the Christian worship of this era. The reasons for the absence of instrumental music from the cult of this period are as complex as those for the previous era. Emphasis on the primacy of vocal music and a concern of Christians to distinguish their worship practices from those of pagans certainly helped to shape worship without instruments—a tradition that would flourish for more than a millennium.

SUMMARY ON 'CHRISTIAN MUSIC' OF THE SECOND AND THIRD CENTURIES

In some respects, the musical developments of this era are symbolic of the basic evolution of the Christian community in the second and third centuries after the death of Christ. It was during this time that Christianity emerged as a recognizable religion, with a distinctive cult, forms of ministry, places of worship, scriptural canon and literature. While still indebted to Judaism, Christianity had clearly separated from Judaism, confronted the Greco-Roman world and gained recognition as a distinctive group by that world.[5]

Similar things could be said about music. It was in this period that identifiable Christian musical forms developed. While closely connected to the lyricism of the previous age, this 'music' was distinctive in text and tone. The debt to

---

[1] James Frederick Mountford and Reginald Winnington-Ingram, 'Music' in *Oxford Classical Dictionary*, p.585.

[2] Hannick, *NGDMM* 4:366.

[3] 'For temperate harmonies are to be admitted ... Chromatic harmonies are, therefore, to be abandoned to immodest revels, and to florid and meretricious music.' (*Paidagogos* 2.4, trans. from Ante-Nicene Fathers 2:249). In commenting on this section, Werner goes further and believes one can reconstruct the actual scale in use by the third century Christians in Alexandria. See *Sacred Bridge* 1:441-445.

[4] McKinnon provides the best compendium of references here in 'The Church Fathers and Musical Instruments'; also useful is Robert Skeris, *Chroma Theoi: On the Origins and Theological Interpretation of the Musical Imagery used by the ecclesiastical writers of the first three centuries, with special reference to the image of Orpheus*, Catholic Church Music Associates, vol. 1 (Alfred Coppenrath, Altötting, 1976).

[5] Harnack, 'Christians as a Third Race', pp.266-278.

Judaism was still evident in the general absence of instruments from the cult, the plethora of *psalmi idiotici* composed in this era, as well as the patterned borrowing of the Davidic psalms. A new alliance with Greco-Roman culture, however, shows itself in the development of metrical hymnody and poetic texts.

The spirit of the primitive community does not seem to be compromised by this new cultural alliance. The acoustic environment suggests that there was still no sharp distinction between the sung and the spoken, no clear division between what we might call the musical and non-musical, nor any denial of the fundamental lyricism of Christian worship. It is, therefore, still difficult to consider music a separate element in the Christian cult at this time. Rather, it was the aural aspect of that cult. This perspective is further reflected in the total absence of any references to special singers, psalmists or cantors at this stage. There is no separate liturgical musician. The whole of worship is musical and to the extent that the worship belonged to the whole assembly, so did the music belong to them.

Alcuin/GROW Joint Liturgical Studies

All cost £3.75 (US $8) in 1992

PATRISTIC STUDIES

GROVE BOOKS LIMITED
Bramcote   Nottingham   NG9 3DS

Grove Liturgical Studies
(32 or 40 pages stapled) £2.75 (US$6) in 1992

ENGLISH TEXTS

8. Hippolytus: A Text for Students, with Translation, Notes and Commentary edited by Geoffrey Cuming (now in fourth impression)

24. Addai and Mari: A Text for Students, with Introduction, Translation, and Notes, edited by Bryan Spinks

29. The Liturgical Portions of the Didascalia, selected, translated and edited by Sebastian Brock and Michael Vasey

OTHER RELEVANT STUDIES in this SERIES

12/13. Worship in the New Testament by C. F. D. Moule (80 pages £5.00) This was the original Lutterworth Ecumenical Study in Worship, now twice reprinted in Grove Liturgical Studies.

15. Essays on Hippolytus, edited by Geoffrey Cuming, with essays on the text (see no. 8 in the Series listed above) by E. C. Whitaker (Baptism), Geoffrey Cuming (Eucharist), and Paul Bradshaw (Ordination)

19. Eucharistic Offering in the Early Church, by R. P. C. Hanson—a re-examination of the doctrine arising from the patristic texts.

31. Eucharistic Sacrifice—The Roots of a Metaphor, by Rowan Williams—a further re-exploration, with reference to Study no. 19 listed above.

36. Liturgical Presidency in the Early Church, by Paul Bradshaw—an expansion of a paper given to the Society for Liturgical Study.

40. Essays on Eucharistic Sacrifice in the Early Church, edited by Colin Buchanan—further papers, relating to nos. 19 and 31 above, from Michael Vasey, Christopher Hancock, David Gregg, Kenneth Stevenson, and Rowan Williams.

45. Fourth Century Anaphoral Construction Techniques, by John Fenwick—an exploration of Eastern roots of eucharistic liturgy.

Alcuin/GROW Joint Liturgical Studies

(48 pages with spine) £3.75 (US$8) in 1992

ENGLISH TEXTS

2. **The Canons of Hippolytus,** edited by Paul Bradshaw—the first English text ever to be available.

13/14. **The Liturgical Portions of the Apostolic Constitutions,** edited by W. Jardine Grisbrooke (double-size, 94pp. £7.50 (US$16))

18. **Irenaeus of Lyon on Baptism and Eucharist,** texts selected, translated, and edited with introduction by David N. Power.

19. **The Testamentum Domini,** edited with translation, introduction and notes by Grant Sperry-White

20. **Origins of the Roman Rite,** edited by Gordon Jeanes

OTHER RELEVANT STUDIES in this SERIES

1. **Daily and Weekly Worship—From Jewish to Christian** by Roger Beckwith (now in second edition)

8. **Essays in Early Eastern Initiation,** edited by Paul Bradshaw

9. **Worship in Ancient Jerusalem,** by John Baldovin

11. **'The Missing Oblation'—The Contents of the Early Antiochene Anaphora',** by John Fenwick (a further exploration of the ground opened in Grove Liturgical Study no. 45 (see facing page)).

22-23. **Foundations of Christian Music: the Music of Pre-Constantinian Christianity** by Edward Foley (double-size, 94pp.£7.50 (US$16)).

ORDERING THESE STUDIES

If you wish to order by post, then stocks are held at the following places, and can be obtained fairly quickly for payment in local currency:

Canada: The Anglican Book Centre, 600 Jarvis Street, Toronto, Ontario, M4Y 2J6
U.S.A.: The Pastoral Press, 225 Sheridan Street, N.W., Washington 20011-1492, USA.
Australia: Ridley College Book Shop, 160 The Avenue, Parkville, Vic. 3052.
New Zealand: Christian Resource Centre, 325 Queen Street, P.O. Box 6561, Auckland.
South Africa: The Rev. M. Coomer, Diocesan College, Camp Grand Road, Rondebosch, 7700, Cape.

For anywhere else in the world, or if any item is out of stock in these places, please order through your local bookseller or direct from Grove Books. In the latter case, please send payment (in sterling or US dollars) with the order, and we will send post-free by surface (or by air for an additional cost).

GROVE BOOKS LIMITED   BRAMCOTE   NOTTINGHAM NG9 3DS

Tel 0602-430786   Fax 0602-220134

THE GROUP FOR RENEWAL OF WORSHIP (GROW)

This Group, originally founded in 1961, has for twenty years taken responsibility for the Grove Books publications on liturgy and worship. Its membership and broad aims reflect a highly reforming, pastoral and missionary interest in worship. Beginning with a youthful evangelical Anglican membership in the early 1970s, the Group has not only probed venturously into the future of Anglican worship, but has also with growing sureness of touch taken its place in promoting weighty scholarship. Thus the list of 'Grove Liturgical Studies' on the facing page shows how, over a twelve-year period, the quarterly Studies added steadily to the material available to students of patristic, reformation and modern scholarly issues in liturgy. In 1986 the Group was approached by the Alcuin Club Committee with a view to publishing the new series of Joint Liturgical Studies, and this series is, at the time of writing, in its sixth year of publication, sustaining the programme with three Studies each year.

Between the old Grove Liturgical Studies and the new Joint Liturgical Studies there is a large provision of both English-language texts and other theological works on the patristic era. These are listed in a systematized way on the next page but one.

Since the early 1970s the Group has had Colin Buchanan as chairman and Trevor Lloyd as vice-chairman.

OTHER GROVE BOOKS PUBLICATIONS ON WORSHIP

GROW puts forward for publication once a quarter a cheaper 'Grove Worship Booklet', which is popular and pastoral in style, 24 pages in length, and £1.60 in sterling price in 1991. The Series has reached no. 122 in mid-1992, and is in numerical continuity with the beginning of the original 'Grove Booklets on Ministry and Worship', of which no. 1 came in December 1971. Recent titles include:

112 **Children in Communion** by Colin Buchanan
113 **But who will Preside?** by Alan Hargrave
114 **Worship in Rural Areas** by David Cutts
115 **Readers and Worship in the Church of England** by Carolyn Headley
116 **Introducing Promise of His Glory** by Trevor Lloyd, Jane Sinclair, Michael Vasey
117 **Multi-Faith Worship and Christian Truth** by David Bookless
118 **Christian initiation in the Anglican Communion** (The Toronto Statement)
119 **Shall We Dance?** by Anne Barton
120 **Methodist and United Reformed Church Worship: Baptism and Eucharist in two 'Free' Churches** by David Kennedy and Phillip Tovey
121 **The Heart of Sunday Worship** by Colin Buchanan
122 **Keeping in Tune with Heaven** by Jane Sinclair
123 **Renewing Daily Prayer** by Christopher Cocksworth and Paul Roberts

Grove Books also publishes a monthly journal, *News of Liturgy,* edited by Colin Buchanan, which is the semi-official channel of information in the Church of England on liturgical subjects. It is sent by air also to subscribers all over the English-speaking world. Postal subscription (without quarterly studies or Booklets) in 1993: £6.00 ($12) inland and surface mail, £8.50 by air overseas (US$17). There is also a quarterly *News of Hymnody.*

For postfree purchases or catalogue information write to Grove Books.

Grove Liturgical Studies

This series began in March 1975, and was published quarterly until 1986. Each title has 32 or 40 pages. Nos. 1, 3-6, and 10 are out of print. Asterisked numbers have been reprinted. Prices in 1992, £2.75 (US$6)

THE ALCUIN CLUB

The Alcuin Club exists to promote the study of Christian liturgy in general, and in particular the liturgies of the Anglican Communion. Since its foundation in 1897 it has published over 130 books and pamphlets. Members of the Club receive some publications of the current year free and others at a reduced rate.

Information concerning the annual subscription, applications for membership and lists of publications is obtainable from the Treasurer, The Revd. T. R. Barker, All Saints' Vicarage, Highlands Road, Runcorn, Cheshire WA7 4PS (Tel. 0928-575 666).

President

The Right Reverend E. W. Kemp, DD, Bishop of Chichester

Committee

The Reverend Canon D. C. Gray, MPhil, PhD, AKC, FRHistS, *Chairman*
The Reverend T. R. Barker, MA, *Treasurer*
The Venerable J. M. M. Dalby, MA, PhD
The Reverend M. R. Dudley, BD, MTh, AKC, DPS, *Secretary*
The Reverend J. R. K. Fenwick, BSc, BA, MTh, STh, PhD
The Reverend Canon R. T. Greenacre, MA
The Reverend Sir Derek Pattinson, MA
The Reverend M. F. Perham, MA
The Reverend P. J. Roberts, BA, PhD
The Reverend K. W. Stevenson, MA, PhD, DD

PUBLISHING PLANS

The Alcuin Club has recently made a three-year arrangement with the Liturgical Press, Collegeville, whereby the old tradition of an annual Alcuin Club major scholarly study will be restored. The first title due under this arrangement is to be published in Autumn 1992: Alastair McGregor, *Fire and Light: The Symbolism of Fire and Light in the Holy Week Services.*

The Joint Liturgical Studies (see the list on a preceding page) have been reduced to three per annum from 1992, and the Alcuin Club subscription now includes the annual publication (as above) and the three Joint Liturgical Studies.

Previous Alcuin Annual titles

Recent Alcuin Titles